The
Frugalista
Files

Natalie P. McNeal

The
Frugalista
Files

How One Woman
Got Out of Debt Without
Giving Up the Fabulous Life

HARLEQUIN®

The Frugalista Files

ISBN-13: 978-0-373-89229-7

© 2011 by Natalie P. McNeal

The names and identifying details of some characters in this book have been changed.

Library of Congress Cataloging-in-Publication Data

McNeal, Natalie P.
The frugalista files: how one woman got out of debt without giving up the fabulous life / Natalie P. McNeal.
p. cm.
ISBN 978-0-373-89229-7 (pbk.)
1. McNeal, Natalie P. 2. McNeal, Natalie P.--Blogs. 3. Finance, Personal--United States--Case studies. 4. Debt--United States--Case studies. 5. Thriftiness--United States--Case studies. 6. Blogs--United States--Case studies. 7. Women--United States--Biography. I. Title.
HG179.M3853 2011
332.024'02--dc22
2010028292

www.eHarlequin.com

Printed in U.S.A.

I dedicate this book to Mom,
Mac, Madison, Kaden, Christian and Coco.
I love you always!

ACKNOWLEDGMENTS

First and foremost, I have to thank everyone who has ever read—and especially who commented on—my blog. I really wrote this book for you. You have listened to my fears and celebrated my triumphs, and I am so humbled. The many conversations that we've had on Twitter (yay, #dealchat), the Facebook group and on my blog have meant the world to me. If anyone had told me that when I started blogging, it would be life changing, I wouldn't have believed them. I am a believer now!

I'd like to thank Harlequin for giving me the opportunity to pursue the dreams of a Frugalista.

Thank you to all my friends and family who have been patient with me throughout this whole book-writing experience. You all are peppered throughout the book, so you know who you are! I'd also like to thank the very patient and loving team of people who have helped me end up here: Ayesha Pande, Marlon Hill, Sarah Pelz, Harriet Bell, Cynthia McNeal and Coco.

CONTENTS

PREFACE

For the majority of my life as a working adult, I've had the nasty gift that keeps on giving: debt. Credit cards, a student loan and a car loan. It shouldn't be a shocker. I was a promiscuous spender, charging trips, dinners, shopping sprees and whatever else on my credit cards. All of this on a print reporter's salary. It wasn't a good look.

I am Natalie P. McNeal, and I created and run my blog Thefrugalista.com, all about living frugal and fabulous.

This book is an up-close look at a very pivotal year in my life: 2008. This book chronicles the year that I decided to beat my debt monster once and for all. It was the year I became a Frugalista, a woman who lives within her budget without sacrificing her fun, fabulous lifestyle. (Yes, it *is* possible!) To stick to my Frugalista mission, I started blogging about the ups and downs of trying to manage my money, career and life over all.

Becoming a Frugalista, hands down, has been one of the best things that I've ever done in life. It started out as a way to pay down debt and manage my money better. Over the course of the year, as I kept blogging and connecting with other people who were going through the same things I was going through or had advice on how to live better, being a Frugalista became empowering. Social media played a big role in helping me connect with the right people to help me on my frugal path.

I wrote this book for everyone who knows they could be doing a little bit or a lot better by their finances but isn't quite sure where to start. I'm just a regular girl who had a vision that she could be debt free. Trust me, if I can be a Frugalista, then you can, too. This book details my journey—the good, the bad and the drama-filled—of trying to reach my goals. I hope it will inspire you to reach your own.

CHAPTER 1

January

DEBTS

xxxxxxxxxxxxxxxxxxxxxxxxxxxxxxxxxxxxxxxx

CREDIT CARDS: $9,785.24

CAR LOAN: $8,600.00

STUDENT LOAN $2,636.00

xxxxxxxxxxxxxxxxxxxxxxxxxxxxxxxxxxxxxxxx

TOTAL DEBTS: $ 21,021.24

xxxxxxxxxxxxxxxxxxxxxxxxxxxxxxxxxxxxxxxx

JANUARY 8

This morning I did the walk of shame. Oh, not *that* kind of walk of shame. The one some women do after leaving some random cat's house in the early morning in yesterday's clothes for all the neighbors to see. No, this walk was a slow, dread-filled stroll in flip-flops, painted toes and pj's to my mailbox. My Visa bill was in my mailbox. My $6,000 Visa bill that showed my shameful, embarrassing, out-of-control spending.

I admit it.

My name is Natalie.

I am a spending slut.

There's more. This isn't the only debt I have. Another credit card shows a $3,785.24 balance due. (Well, that was my balance at the beginning of the week. In the time it took me to walk from my mailbox to the 1-bedroom apartment that I call home, the bill probably jumped an additional $75, thanks to interest.) As for savings (I use the term loosely…), I have about $1,000 in a savings account that I use to cover bills.

My emotions about this mess range from feeling pretty pissy to being downright scared. I work hard. Real hard. I daresay, I'm a working stiff. Don't I deserve those mani-pedis? Why shouldn't I buy those marked-down Kate Spade shoes? On the other hand, how did I become this crazy, out-of-control walking ATM machine?

I thought that when you're depressed, you crawl into bed and sleep for weeks. But I couldn't sleep a wink last night.

Every year I say I'm going to be better about my spending and my bills. I worry that I'm starting to sound like a broken record. Enough, all ready. I can't keep this act up. When will my credit card debt be gone for good?

The worst part of it is that I don't even know where the money's been spent. What is on these credit cards? And what in the hell do I have to show for it?

I won't. I will not. I cannot keep this act up. This is the year I will get *really* serious about my money. I can't keep living like this: professional, broke and in debt. I am not living like an extra on *Sex and the City*. I am living like the workin', frontin' POOR!

JANUARY 9

Is there something wrong with me? Not only is my spending out of control, but I'm stuck. I've been at the same job for almost 8 years. I live in the same 1-bedroom apartment I first rented when I was 24 years old. The rent, which started at $818 a month, is now $995. My apartment complex went condo, so I'm one of the few renters left. The cheap, ugly linoleum floor is cracked, and my landlord is in no rush to replace it.

How did I end up here? Why do I always feel like I'm slogging through an endless Florida swamp when it comes to my life?

I was sure that by the time I was 32 years old, I'd be married, have a top-notch job at a major newspaper and be nominated (at least once) for a Pulitzer Prize.

Being stretched so thin—financially and emotionally—got me here, melted on my couch. And while sitting on my couch, I noticed the new rug, coffee table, TV stand and fake-assed tree hanging in my living room, all courtesy of a late fall spending spree. Right before the Youngster came to visit, I started sprucing up the home, thinking a hip house would make me look more professional and together. It was about time I had "big girl" furniture, not a footlocker as a television stand…or so I rationalized. I mean, at least, he has an excuse for his bachelor pad—he's still in his 20s.

At age 31, I'm not poised to jump the broom any time soon. I'm dating a man 7 years my junior. Okay, so he lives in New York City. We've been "seeing each other" for the last 3 months. The Youngster works full-time and is finishing up his undergraduate degree. Damn, I'm a cougar. Well, maybe a puma…I don't troll bars in tacky leopard print dresses, looking for young boys. We instant message each other. He's the one who got me into Facebook. For Christmas, I FedExed the Youngster an adorable $100 Sean John jacket. He sent me a Tiffany silver heart bracelet, which arrived on Christmas eve. I wear it every day, and every time I look at it, I smile. It's been a while since I got some hardware from the male species. So sweet.

He came to visit in December, right before the holidays, and took my mother, who was in town, and me to P.F. Chang's for dinner. It's one of her favorite restaurants. Said the maternal about the Youngster: "He's very polite. You can tell he was 'raised.'" My mother is from the South and is a retired schoolteacher. Having "raising" is like saying he is the Second Coming. Yep. She was hooked. He slept on the couch that night and she slept in my bed. Talk about family togetherness! He doesn't complain about me, either. Jeez. You date some guys, and they always find a problem with you: weight, hair, personality. He is a hand holder. Reads my articles in the newspaper, even when I am bored with them. He sent me flowers just because… just because I am breathing. He says, "Let's think long term."☺ He acts smitten. *Me gusta.*

He's relatively easy to talk to and low maintenance. I also like that he's not a drinker. A lot of guys my age are budding bitter drunks. Older men…hmmm…they can be a project. Everyone my age is realizing that things aren't quite what we had expected them to be. We assumed that by 30, we were going to be something special: be rich, have a Ph.D. or be an extraterrestrial. Quite honestly, dating in my age pool can be a hassle. Despite the long distance, it's kinda nice dating someone younger because the Youngster is still optimistic about life. I, on the other hand, know I have a good life, but I also know that this can't be as good as it gets. This is what's freaking me out—this *can't* be as good as it gets.

We'll see how it goes with him. I enjoy our time together. When we're together. When he visits, we have a ball and he pays for everything: nice dinners, Miami Heat games. But for the most part, it's a virtual relationship. I am tolerating the distance for now, to see if it's worth it. But I know the only way the Youngster and I can make it work is if we're in the same city. I'm more than willing to ditch my job.

My work life is…hmmm…stagnant. When I mention that I'm a reporter at the *Miami Herald*—a well-respected paper in the middle of one of the sexiest and newsiest markets, a paper that's won plenty of Pulitzers and is a feeder to the *Washington Post* and the *New York Times*—trust me, it sounds impressive. But really, how prestigious is the suburban office in the Everglades, next to a Cracker Barrel and a car dealership?

I took the job in the suburban office, believing I'd be there for just 2 years before being recruited by the *Washington Post* or moved to the business desk, which is where I really want to work. That was almost 8 years ago. Have I heard from the *Post*? Well, I did get a once-over by them at a career conference. Um, yeah. That was the end of that. I still cover city commission meetings, daily shootings and news conferences in the burbs. On weekends I cover car crashes on Alligator Alley, the road that connects east and west in South Florida. So much for *Miami Vice.*

I am bored out of my mind. My salary sucks. What I write about isn't sexy or glamorous. It's a grind. Everyone at work wonders why I haven't left. I kind of wonder why, too, but then I remember the few job offers I've gotten since working there: more local reporter coverage of city commissions. With newspapers going the way of the pony express, finding a new job that I want is a hot mess. It's more of the same type of work. It's hard to transition to being a business reporter when most of your clips are local news.

I reread the above and feel even more depressed. I don't leave my low-paying, dead-end job, because I need the money to pay my rent, car and school loans, and to bring down my credit card bills. And I have a habit called eating. I can't make a dent in paying off my credit cards, because I use them to charge all of my life's necessities— drinks and dinners out, hair salon visits, a magazine rack in an attempt to make my bunny pad look nicer, etc. And ranting about it doesn't seem to do any good, either. The sad part is, I pay my debts on time, and I'm still broke. Paying bills on time means I pay the minimum amount due on my cards for a *really* long time. What's the point of a good credit score if you live from paycheck to paycheck?

I have to try something new. I can't go through the rest of my life broke and in debt.

JANUARY 11

I sat myself down and forced myself to do the math. I make $44,000 a year and take home $1,200 every 2 weeks after health care and my 6 percent 401(k) contribution (and yes, I'm vested in my 401(k) and proud of it!). My rent at $995 and my car loan at $313 per month take care of one $1,200 check. My student loan is $50 per month, which doesn't sound like a lot. The thing is, it should have been paid off this year, but when I got my car, I couldn't handle the $129 student loan and the car loan, so I consolidated my payments. I added a few more years' worth of payments on my student loan, adding more interest on the bill. The original debt of $10,600 wasn't even that bad, and I'm still paying on it. That darn student loan has become like a mortgage payment, a longtime payment that is hard to fathom getting rid of.

I have to take a break. This is too painful....

JANUARY 11, CONTINUED

How did I wind up here, anyway? I have a career, a college education—this wasn't supposed to happen to me....

I can't help but think that I never would have been in such bad debt if it weren't for my first car loan. As a journalism student in D.C., interning at various newspapers, I needed a car. My mother and I saw a TV commercial offering a lease on a Mazda Protégé for less than $200 per month. Sounded like a great deal. A cousin with his own business agreed, saying that buying a car is a bad investment. Leasing is better, he told us.

I had a savings account with money saved from my internship, so I put down $1,500 and my mother paid the car loan. For some reason, though, the car loan was more than $200. And we never questioned it. (I know. I know.) At the time, it cost only about $12 to fill up the car with gas. I was rolling.

Since the car was leased, I could drive it only 15,000 miles a year. Well, after several trips to New York and Philadelphia to party with friends, and driving to and from internships in Dallas and Miami, it would be an understatement to say I went over the allotted mileage. I went way, way, way over the mileage.

And Washington is no place for a new car. Parking garages were too snug and expensive, so I parked the car on the street. Well, that's okay if you know how to parallel park. If you successfully do back in, getting out of a tight parking space can be even more difficult. Dents. Dings. Scrapes. Chips. Dimples. If there was such a thing as car abuse, surely my Mazda would have been taken into automobile protective services. I would have been cuffed, forced to walk the perp walk and made to face the judge and jury.

When the lease was up, the car was a wreck. It was cheaper

for me to buy the car than to try to fix it up or pay the overage on the mileage. So, after spending thousands to rent it for 3 years, I paid for it over another 4 years at the monthly rate of $224. And because I was officially grown up and out of college, Mom's gravy train had come to an end.

Driving that eyesore was an embarrassment. It was such a piece of junk that some friends wouldn't ride in the car with me. ("Why don't I pick *you* up?") I was afraid to send it through the car wash for fear that one of the headlights would fall off. I (stupidly) paid $200 to a guy who promised he could smooth out the dents with a crowbar. Working in the parking lot of a strip mall, the dude made things worse by using gold lamé spray paint to pimp my car and "fix" the scrapes on my once champagne-colored ride. I drove that miserable clunker until it couldn't go another mile. Literally. It was in such bad shape that I had to pay to have it towed from my apartment to the junkyard.

Having learned my leasing lesson, it was time to buy my first car. I wanted and could afford a Honda Civic, but my mother and my brother said no. They were tired of me being the girl with the battered starter car. I mean, my first car was named the Protégé. They wanted me in a more mature car. Warned my mother: "What if you want to have a family? You won't be able to fit them into a Honda Civic."

I thought about those things, too. But honestly, I just didn't think my family wanted to ride around in an entry-level car with me when they visited. They wanted me upgraded to where I should be at my age. They knew I was in no position to buy a house. The next best thing was a decent/respectable/professional ride.

So, of course, I listened to them, visions of babbling, cooing babies in the backseat. I bought a used Honda Accord for $15,000 and put $2,000 down. My monthly payments came to $313 over a 5-year period. Between the taxes and interest, this car will end up costing about $20,000. Had I bought the Civic, my payments would have been closer to $200 a month.

Here I am, 3 years later, still paying $313 per month on a 4-door sedan. And no gurgling babies.

What did I learn from all this? Never, ever listen to your family—mother, brother, cousin, step aunt's sister's cousin's brother-in-law—when buying a car. My brother and mom don't have my bank account.

JANUARY 12

Okay, so car and rent. Where does the rest of my money go?

As a reporter for the *Miami Herald*, I drive to crime scenes, news conferences, city commission meetings and courthouses. I have to fill up my tank twice a week at $30 a pop. Okay, so I'm not the best at keeping receipts and turning them in at work for reimbursement. I can't even lie. When I first took the job at the *Miami Herald*, I didn't even get reimbursed for my moving expenses from my old job in North Carolina to Miami, er, the suburban swamp. Why? BECAUSE I DIDN'T FILL OUT THE PAPERWORK TO BE REIMBURSED. I paid for my own moving expenses because I was so embarrassed that I didn't fill out the paperwork in time. Ugh.

Car Insurance: $110 a month

Renter's Insurance: $500 a year (I mean, I live in South Florida, where hurricanes and other acts of nature are a way of life. I didn't want to see my belongings washed away in a storm.)

Dry Cleaning: About $60 every 3 months (I do love silk. Silk shirts. Silk dresses. [Naturally, I only buy them on sale.] South Florida is sunny and steamy. Silk and steamy don't mix very well. When you sweat, the armpits of white and beige silk garments turn, shall we say, a very mellow yellow. One wear, and those bargains are off to the dry cleaner. Silk blouses on sale + repeated dry cleaning = no bargain.)

I'm a big believer in taking classes to advance my, ahem, "career." Last year I flew to New York to take a crash Flash course for journalists. (The course set me back $400. The airplane ticket to New York was $200. Food and cabs were about $100. In all, the trip was a

$700 affair. Eek! I "saved" money by staying with my friend Carly.) And I didn't understand a single thing the instructor said after the first 2 hours. My classmates groaned and grumbled because I asked so many questions, effectively making me the class jerk. I majored in journalism, not computer science. How am I supposed to understand how to manipulate vector graphics? What the hell is a vector graphic, anyway? Flash is evil. There, I said it. I ran out of class to meet my friends for dinner. We feasted and drank that evil Flash class away. I was scarred from the experience. How are you going to teach a print reporter one of the most cryptic software programs or whatever it's supposed to be (I didn't stay in class, so I'm not sure)? It was cruel and unusual punishment!

I spent another $600 on online content for a website course. At least this time I didn't have to travel. I attended class once a week from my dining room, or as I like to call it, my office. My place is too small for both a dining room table and a computer desk. The computer desk won out. (A girl's got to have her priorities, and let's face it, I'm not much of a cook.) I launched my own website, to showcase my clips, costing me $1,200. I paid cash for it and basically cut my savings account in half. It was for my career, after all. I thought it was gorgeous. All the job recruiters said it was nice. But did Natalie get a job? Hell no! Natalie still click clacks at her messy desk in the South Florida swamp, er, suburbs.

There's the annual journalism convention that I try to attend. That's about $1,000 for a new suit, travel and hotel (even sharing with a roommate). I always thought it was worth it to network, but I wonder if it's really worth paying to network in an industry that's not growing…?

The rest, about $100 to $200 per month, goes to paying off my credit cards. Paying them off, I s'pose, wouldn't be such a problem if I didn't keep charging my life: my Thai food addiction, my twice-monthly hair appointments, my kick-it weekend trips with my friends, my manicures and pedicures, my clothes and shoes.

I want to be debt free. Really, I do. But here I am…over $20,000 in debt and the hole just seems to be getting deeper and wider. When I think about it, I realize I'm almost half of my income in debt for past transgressions. Le sigh.

JANUARY 13

Okay, so I have issues with money. The only way I can think of to get out of this problem is to stop. Stop spending money. But will not spending money get me out of debt? And after a lifetime of binge spending, can I possibly rein it in?!

JANUARY 14

The lightbulb went off last night. Being a spending slut is ruining my life. I asked myself, "What's the opposite of debt?" The answer: no debt. And there's only one way to get out of debt: Stop putting out. Stop spending. Stop buying. Stop consuming. Stop shopping. Stop charging. Stop wanting more stuff. Being a spending slut is ruining my life. I am not going to buy anything for 1 month. Nothing. One whole month. Starting February 1—the first day of the shortest month and my birthday month. My credit cards will go in my desk drawer. I will pay my rent, my school loan, my car loan and my credit cards. I will buy food only to be cooked at home and gasoline. With cash. Yes, that's it. I am going to boycott buying crap.

JANUARY 15

I can't believe I'm going to "boycott buying crap." Me? Did some finance fairy get into my diary yesterday and write that? I love shopping. And by shopping, I don't mean window-shopping. I mean spending money. I mean wandering through stores, trying on clothes and shoes for hours, and then taking my favorites to the cash register and walking out with shopping bags. I mean having my hair and nails done regularly. I love to go out to bars and to restaurants. I love to travel.

For as long as I can remember, my mother got her hair professionally done every Friday night by Leonard, our family hairstylist. Every *other* Friday night, Leonard styled my hair as well. My mother was always complimented on how nice her hair looked wherever we went. Whenever I got my hair done, it would shake and shine and smell awesome. My friends at school would marvel at the body in my hair. Attempts to create a similar look at home were never quite successful, so why bother? Just spend the money and look good. BEAUTY COSTS!

My mother and I went shopping every Saturday morning while my dad slept or played golf. We went to T.J. Maxx, Marshalls and other discount stores. We either put fashionable items on layaway ("Oh, I can wear those designer jeans to school in 4 weeks!") or had to make a payment on merchandise already on layaway. Credit cards have made buying things on layaway pretty rare these days. But back in the day, layaway, or an installment plan, was a common way to purchase an item without paying the entire cost all at once. The store "laid the item away" until the customer paid for the whole thing, usually over weeks or months. With cash. Layaway was how I was taught to shop. With layaway, you always put up your cute stuff. No one put underwear or long johns on layaway in my home.

When filling out the forms, my mother would always write: "Do not send a reminder to home address." When we got back from our Saturday morning shopping jaunts, we waited until my dad was sound asleep on the brown couch downstairs, and then we brought the shopping bags into the house, so he wouldn't see how much damage we'd done.

My mother taught me to shop by label—Liz Claiborne and Calvin Klein were like personal friends—and for bargains. I once scored a pair of $100 Girbaud pants (brown with gold pinstripes) for $5. Mom was so proud! She taught her baby well. I remember wearing them to school, and I kept the tag on them, showing the pants off to my friends, who marveled. They were *only* $5!

What she didn't realize was that she was creating a mall monster. One year I wanted a Gucci bag for Christmas. Instead, my mother bought me a fake one and tried to pass it off as the real thing. I ripped into her. "I know my brands. How dare you buy a phony beige, not tan, plastic bag with interlocking *O*s instead of 2 *G*s?" I refused to wear it and tossed it on a closet shelf. As if I didn't know Occi from Gucci!

The next year she bought me a real Gucci bag.

I was so proud of that slim, chic Gucci bag. I wore it for special occasions, school dances and parties. I even wore it on my eighth grade graduation trip to Illinois's state capital, Springfield. In the class photo, there I am in the front row—even though I was taller than most of the other girls and boys at that age and belonged in the back—making sure that my Gucci bag gets a photo op. A Gucci bag is meant to be seen.

By the time I reached high school, I was a full-out fashionista. My next name-brand bag was Coach, complete with my initials. I wanted Girbaud jeans but couldn't see why I should wait a season or two for them to make it to the off-price stores. I wanted them. Immediately. Department stores carried exactly what I wanted, when I wanted it. I upgraded and started shopping at Marshall Field's and other downtown Chicago stores where nothing was discounted. Among my coveted high school buys: $90 Girbaud jeans and $75 Guess jeans.

Favorite brands, like Benetton or Esprit, never showed up at off-price stores. Once, when I coveted a had-to-have $50 Benetton sweater, I hit my father up for some extra loot. He thought I was going to buy a bunch of things with that money, and when he found out that I spent $50 on 1 sweater, he went into one of his standard tirades. "All you want to do is shop," he ranted. "When will you learn that you don't spend every dime you have? When are you going to start saving for a rainy day?" Blah, blah, blah, blah…. Why give me money if you're going to be upset with how I spend it? I didn't ask him for any clothing money after that. The lesson I learned? Not to ask him for cash, because I didn't want him foaming at the mouth about how I spent it.

My dad has a different view of money than my mother and me. My family has lived in the same house since I was 1 and I don't remember us ever buying as much as a new chair. When new flooring was needed in the kitchen, my dad insisted on wack linoleum, rather than the more expensive tile. My parents never refinanced their house. Our cars were sensible—an Accord and a Ford Taurus.

The latter came with Dad's sales job. He thought it was ridiculous to pay someone else to cut the grass when I or my brother could do it for free. Oh, and that included pruning the bushes, edging the lawn and spreading insecticides on the weeds.

While Dad might have ruled the roost when it came to household spending, Mom and I paid no mind to his frugal—aw, let's just say it, cheap—ways at the malls and stores. We went shopping. Illicit shopping with my mom was a fun release from my father's constant ranting. Especially when he was on the road for work. No sneaking shopping bags into the house. No grouch asking how much money we spent today.

Most families are sad when a parent has to travel for business. We were thrilled. While the cat's away, the mice will shop. My parents are divorced now. No shocker on that one. It's better that way. Opposites shouldn't attract.

I like nice stuff. I wish I had the budget for it. I buy my clothing on sale or at a discount, but I can't keep acting like I'm being kept by two working professionals. I have one professional income, not two. My rent is more expensive than the old mortgage on my family home. It doesn't work to try to shop within my means. I just don't think I have enough means, because I owe everyone. I work to pay others. I am not working to save. Ugh. What's even more embarrassing, I wore higher-end clothes as a kid than I do now! I need a sponsor! Let's just say that the Gucci bag that my mother bought me was my first and LAST Gucci.

I feel like it's the first days of a new diet. I'm energized, empowered and determined to follow the rules and eat only small quantities of healthy food. Or, spend small amounts…only on necessities.

I can't do this alone. I need help. I need support. Yeah, it's like a diet. I need to share my thoughts and feelings with other spendthrifts like me. I need the financial equivalent of Weight Watchers, a group to share my money gains and losses with.

JANUARY 16

So what does a writer do when she has an idea? She writes about it! This morning I approached the business desk's editor and told her about my idea for getting out of debt and taking control of my finances. And writing about my new frugal (that word *so* doesn't sound like me) ways in a blog would make me publicly accountable for my spending and saving. She loved the idea!

I pitched it as a blog about my boycott on spending. That's right. I am going cold turkey with the spending—for a month. I got it approved and I am going to get a freelance check for doing extra work. Yay! I am so happy I got the green light.

The bosses on the business desk (heh-heh, I knew I'd get myself on that business desk somehow) hated the first name I picked for it—and passed on "Miser McNeal." In Miami, everything has a heavy Spanish and Latin influence, so when I added "ista" to "frugal" and suggested The Frugalista Files, they gave me the go-ahead. Yay!

JANUARY 18

The Youngster is in town! He flew down to Miami and we are going to Disney World. My friends are impressed that we are going on a trip together. It's a step forward! So far, so good. We've been chatting since August; the relationship became official last October. But I have to be honest—we've only seen each other in person for a total of 9 days. Still, I'm taking this relationship thing as seriously as I can.

We are driving the 3 hours up to Disney and checking out Universal Studios, the four-fingered pimp, I mean, Mickey Mouse, and just doing the overgrown kid thing. I'm excited. All I have to do is sit through one of those god-awful time-share condo pitches that I have no plans of signing up for, and we are golden with Disney tickets.

He offered to pay for everything, but I insisted on splitting expenses. I'm an independent woman!

Also, some of his cousins are in Orlando, so we are going to visit them. I'm excited. I like getting to know people better.

So, we'll see where things go. Also, I need a break from work and stress, and this young guy thing seems to be one of the few things that are making sense right about now.

JANUARY 19

On the way to Orlando I told the Youngster about my Frugalista plan and he was totally on board. Said he'd try it the following month, too. I was a little surprised and excited. He does the online web-producing thing. Makes more money than I do. But he's down with cutting spending, too. Yay! We're a team.

Universal Studios was super fun. I love that mummy ride. I screamed. Yeah, I'm a scaredy-cat. He was there for me to hold on to. I like that feeling. I'm such a girl's girl, but it's nice to have a guy around.

Today we went to hang out with the head rat in charge, Mickey. Since living in Florida, I have been to Disney World just once. I remember going when I was like 8 years old on a family trip, but I've taken only one other trip as an adult. Dude knew all the words to all the songs in the exhibits. How adorable. I'm such a predator, dating a younger guy who is a Disney fan! It's raining pretty bad here today. We dodged the raindrops as best we could. It's all good. No complaints from either one of us.

JANUARY 20

We hung out with his cousins today. An adorable family with young kids. I spent *way* too much time playing with the little ones. His cousin was sweet and made us breakfast. I accidentally crashed into her mailbox, scratching up my car. Meh. I let the Youngster drive on the way home. Nice to have someone to turn the keys over to. Nice to sleep without the lights on. (Yes, I am a grown woman, but I am still afraid of the dark. I can't sleep in the dark by myself. When the Youngster comes to visit, the lights are out.)

JANUARY 21

And poof. He's gone. I hate goodbyes.

JANUARY 25

Last night I had my last supper with my college alum friends and a coworker. It was so cool. Everyone said they were excited for me and couldn't wait to see how I was going to do with the no-buy month. Most of my friends are attorneys or married to attorneys. They (or their spouses) make much more than I do, so I was a little bit surprised how psyched they were for me. Then again, they all have their or their husband's law school loans to pay off, so I guess they understood. Talking with them made me feel better, even though our meals were $30 apiece. I like shrimp and it's costly.

JANUARY 31

EEEEK! On my last day of credit freedom, I am feverishly trying to get my work done so I can do a mall run, get a mani-pedi and browse the sale racks for one last fix. At the nail salon, my tech said that business was pretty slow. I let her know it was about to get slower because I won't be in for a month. I swear, I think she did the best pedicure I've had from her—ever. Nat the Meal Ticket is checking out for a bit. Someone else can be her paymaster. LOL

I'm freaking out a bit. I can't believe I'm going to put myself out there like that with a work blog. I like most of my coworkers, but it's not like me to put it all out there. What (else) will they think of me at the office? Only in a newsroom can you write about your deepest fears—FOR WORK! Most of my close friends don't work at the office, and now here I am, about to write about my money woes for a month. Operation Broke Chick on blast.

I'm a little worried about what people are going to think, but I'm a little more worried about how I feel about myself. Not so great.

CHAPTER 2

February

```
DEBTS

xxxxxxxxxxxxxxxxxxxxxxxxxxxxxxxxxxxx

CREDIT CARDS:    $9,550.63

CAR LOAN:        $8,320.76

STUDENT LOAN:    $2,587.12


xxxxxxxxxxxxxxxxxxxxxxxxxxxxxxxxxxxx

TOTAL DEBTS:  $ 20,458.51

xxxxxxxxxxxxxxxxxxxxxxxxxxxxxxxxxxxx
```

FEBRUARY 1

Today is the first day of my new frugal life. My no-buy month has begun. I wrote a column for the paper about the challenge. It was a hit with 9 pages of comments, and my post made the website's home page! Yay! *Ego stroke! Ego stroke!* Everyone at work thinks that all I'm going to do is get men to take me on dates and buy me things to supplement my no-buy month. The nerve of them. I am an independent woman. I don't need a man to get through this month. I am spoken for, anyway. The Youngster is my man. He takes me out... monthly. So there!

And 2 radio stations called to interview me! Isn't that crazy? I can't believe they are calling me. I never get interviewed for any of my work. Bit of a buzz in the office. The Boss Lady patted me on the back and said she was proud of me. Yay! And she didn't say anything about me going to another department, the business desk, to get it done. Phew!

Since I couldn't go out and spend any money, I went home after work and tried to get my life in order. Amazing what you find when you do a little housekeeping! While cleaning countertops and throwing out old bills and junk mail, I found a $50 check dated January 4 from my mother under a stack of old *Newsweek* magazines. Every year my mom comes to stay with me for at least a month during the Christmas holidays. During one of our shopping expeditions, she spotted a dress and a blouse that were perfect for her and cost only $50. Since the store wouldn't take an out-of-state check, I wrote the check, and my mom wrote me a check to reimburse me. I forgot all about it.

I walked (free!) to the bank near my home and deposited the check. Lesson learned: paper on a desk is evil. Who knows? There may be more money lurking about. This Frugalista stuff might not be so bad, after all.

People are already reading my blog! A reader emailed me saying she was going to join me on my journey. She said she wasn't going to do her mother–daughter run to go shopping this weekend. OMG! My mom and I weren't the only ones? Other mothers and daughters bond with a good trip to the local department store? I thought that was kind of cool, getting an email from someone about what I'm up to. When you're a reporter, you tend to get comments about other people's lives and what you wrote about them. I am not a columnist, so it's kind of new to get feedback about my life. I emailed her back, wishing her the best. Strength in numbers, *chica!*

FEBRUARY 2

Everyone says one way to save money is to cook at home, so instead of making reservations, my friend Vivian and I headed to the supermarket to buy food. I am new to this cooking business. I can tell you the price of a good pair of jeans, but I have no idea how much food is supposed to cost. (Okay, shoot me.) Look, I know seafood isn't cheap, but I didn't expect to spend $25 on 3½ pounds of crab!

3½ POUNDS CRAB	$ 24.46
1 BOTTLE OF WINE	$ 7.99
1 BOTTLE OF	
VINAIGRETTE DRESSING	$ 2.29
2 SWEET POTATOES	$ .99
1 BAG OF PREWASHED SALAD	$ 2.99
xxxxxxxxxxxxxxxxxxxxxxxxxxxxxxxxxxxxxxxxxxxxxxxxxxxx	
TOTAL	$ 38.72
xxxxxxxxxxxxxxxxxxxxxxxxxxxxxxxxxxxxxxxxxxxxxxxxxxxx	

It was really nice chez moi with my friend, just chitchatting and catching up, but my share was 20 bucks! And I learned a few things:

1. *I like baked sweet potatoes. And they are super easy to make.*
2. *I have to keep a budget and menu in mind when going grocery shopping. And stick to it.*
3. *Potlucks might be a good idea.*
4. *Eating in = leftovers. I had salad left over for the next day.*

Vivian is the first person I met when I moved here. Actually, we met in Washington, D.C., at the NBA All-Star Weekend. One of our mutual friends invited us both to party that weekend. We had a great time—we went to Jay-Z's party (amazing!) and hit the shops together. After partying that weekend, I would see her at the parties in South Florida and we started hanging out. When you are single and like to travel and kick it, you tend to bond across state lines. She works in customer service. We share a love of nightlife. We kicked it at the Essence Music Festival. We pool our "party capital" together and always try to go to the best events with the best men. It works. She's a close friend, but this is like only the second time that she's ever been to my place. I never invite people over, because I am always in the streets, hanging out. Who wants to party in a 1-bedroom?

"Look at Natalie. You're all grown up," Vivian said. The last time she was over to the apartment, I was still representing with the footlocker as a TV stand. I must say, my decorations are pretty cute, even if I should have paid cash for them. At least I can see where some of my money went. Vivian met the Youngster the first time he was in town, when we all went to a University of Miami game. She's a big fan. She thinks I need to take it day by day, though. I agree. I can be a bit demanding.☺

FEBRUARY 3

I had a love affair with George this morning. George Foreman, that is. It's Sunday and I had to work today, so George and I grilled some chicken breasts. I packed the chicken, some salad and an apple in a bag. It had to last me through the day. I like this cooking healthy stuff, but it sure isn't as filling as eating out. What do restaurants put in their food, anyway? The good thing about packing a lunch is that I can eat at my desk and get my work done faster.

Super Bowl party tonight. Was worried that I wouldn't have time to eat before the party, which is at the Dolphins' stadium. I love a good Super Bowl jam. Lots of menfolk and down here in Miami is where all the athletes live. Everyone had to pay for their own food, and stadium food is sooooo expensive, though. Not for me. (Anymore.) Ate before I went to meet up with Vivian and the rest of the girls.

Vivian's friend Gary said he read my blog. Oops! Exposed!

He was smiling. "I'm making sure you don't spend any money! I'm watching you!" Gary said.

Gah! I'm in a bubble! Even at a Super Bowl party. He bought my drink, though.☺

FEBRUARY 4

Yeah, so I'm no Julia Child. Tonight's dinner was a mix of celery and peanut butter, with a side of salsa and tortilla chips. This cooking coordination is challenging. No problem eating my breakfast at home and bringing my lunch to work. But when the night falls, I'm not the best at organizing meals. So much other stuff to think about other than whipping up a warm meal. I take something out of the freezer and forget to cook it. Or forget to take something out of the freezer, then regret not having something to cook. Thawing food in the nuker is a production.

In an effort to cut back on my electricity bill, I'm definitely going to turn off the lights tonight before I go to sleep. Ugh! Ugh!

1. *I find it easier to roll into bed than to remember to shut down every light in the place.*
2. *The lights are like my protector. A smarter woman would have a night-light, but that's so childish. I'm a grown woman. If I get a night-light, that means I really have a sleeping-in-the-dark problem. Then again, being spooked of the dark is pretty childlike.*

FEBRUARY 5

My stomach growled the whole darn day. I think I'm starving myself. I am always hungry. I need some lard. Some special oils to stick to my ribs. Whatever they put in that take-out Chicken Basil…mmm. I know I'm cooking "sensible meals" like the ones I see in magazines. But why does my cooking leave me sooooo hungry?

FEBRUARY 6

The Youngster got a new job as a sports editor that pays much more (his salary is even *more* than mine now!) and he's the mini-boss man. He's moving on up. But our relationship doesn't seem to be. It's getting a bit odd. He can be reached only online via chat and has little time to talk on the phone.

Yeah, I know he's busy with school and the new job, but we aren't talking as much as we used to. By the time he's done working, I'm passed out asleep. I don't get it. Since the Disney trip, we just haven't been in sync. I'm not sure if he's stressed about his new job or if it's something I said. We're meant to see each other in NOLA in 2 weeks. Maybe things will improve then?

FEBRUARY 7

I've been doing this no-buy thing for a week now. I'm bringing in my lunch, so I don't leave for lunch during the day. My bank account is doing okay, too. I'm so used to seeing my account go down every day. But it's gone down only a few dollars since last week! It's like it's…I daresay…stable. I just thought that the money always leaves until your next payday. I never thought of actually KEEPING MONEY in a checking account. I keep money in a SAVINGS account, but not a checking account. That's crazy. Maybe I can have stability in both?

I'm working on the cooking thing. I know that not cooking has made me less marketable in the dating scene. Men like a woman who can cook. Heck, I like women and men who can cook, so they can cook for me! My mom can cook. I love it. I wish men valued women who can edge the lawn, because then I'd be "the woman!"

At least I have more time to cook now that I'm not shopping and going out. Tonight I made some salmon (nuked it in the microwave with a little butter, seasoned salt, garlic salt and cayenne pepper). On the side, I stir-fried some asparagus with a little bit of garlic and olive oil. And it was good! Need to ask Mom for some quick and easy recipes. If I like my cooking, why didn't I start cooking earlier?

FEBRUARY 9

Last night my friend/coworker Miguel took me and one of our new coworkers, Teresa, out for drinks. Both Miguel and Teresa are editors at the paper. The Boss Lady asked me to look out for the new editor. She wants me to be the cultural ambassador for the workplace. I've worked there so long, I might as well be part of the furniture, I suppose. Sometimes I feel like the new newsroom social committee. It doesn't pay enough, though. But I digress....

I told Miguel about my new role as ambassador and we all agreed to meet up and have drinks. He picks the coolest places. We met in the Design District. So happy he sponsored it. I mean, he has a corporate card. I sure as hell don't!

FEBRUARY 10

Plan was to meet the Youngster in New Orleans next weekend, just a $200 plane ride from Florida. He'll be attending the NBA All-Star Game for his new job. I bought the ticket, even though he offered to pay for it after a mini-fight. And then I canceled the trip when he made it clear that he wouldn't be able to get me into any of the parties, because he would be working and wouldn't have a hookup.

I'm skeptical. To say the least. What sports journalist doesn't get hookups to the events? Pimp the company name? Hmmm. He never acted like that before. This is the same guy who brought his work to Miami so we could hang out together. He always tried to make a way and now he's super busy? This is the one month we were supposed to see each other twice. If we are going to do this relationship thing, we need to really do it. I'm not about to meet him in New Orleans and then spend the weekend by myself. Plus, the trip would have been an opportunity to spend Valentine's Day together! Not amused. *So* not amused.

FEBRUARY 11

I'm starting to take this Frugalista thing seriously. Today's project: find a credit card with a lower interest rate—if I have to pay off a huge debt, I may as well minimize the interest, right?

I looked on Bankrate.com, a personal finance site that keeps track of rates offered on everything from credit cards to mortgages. I found a credit card with a lower rate than the one I've been paying and applied for a new card. I got approved (oh, the irony of having a good credit rating when you're totally broke!) and transferred over the balance of one of my higher-rate credit cards to the new one. This new card has a 4.99 percent interest rate for the life of the balance, *much* lower than the 11.9 percent I was paying before. I will be able to pay off the balance more quickly because I will be paying less on interest. Frugalista tip: Be sure to check your credit card interest rate—there may be a better rate out there, which will help you minimize your extra charges!

FEBRUARY 12

I woke up early to go on the local CBS show to talk about the Frugalista thing. Jeez. I had to shop in my closet, which is for the best. I would have loved to buy a new outfit or at least a new shirt. I remember when I interviewed P. Diddy a few years earlier, I bought a new shirt for the interview. (Okay, so my job *is* cool sometimes.) You can't be shabby at a Diddy interview. The guy wears shiny suits, for Pete's sake.

But, with the no-buy month, I can't do any of it. No retail confidence boost. Gah. I have to make do with me, just as I am. It was my first time at the CBS studio down here. It's like Fort Knox, getting into that jammie. You have to check in before they let you park. My suburban office is *nothing* like that. At the studio I got signed in and waited to be called in. While I waited, during every commercial break, the anchors whipped out the makeup. I usually don't even wear foundation. Gah!

The interview went well, I think. I got a few emails from friends who saw it. Sometimes I just think people are so excited to see someone they know on TV that they aren't even thinking, *Jeez, she's bad with a budget.* I've gotten a few offers for some dates, too, from men who read my column in the paper or saw me on television. Is being broke a turn-on? Heehee.

FEBRUARY 13

So, my friend at work arranged for me to be on the *Miami Herald*'s web show. I woke up early to wash my hair so it was fresh for the day. My hair is thick. Clearly, my mother mated with a wolf. I shouldn't have waited until the last minute to wash my hair. I was due at the studio before daylight. I should have done it the night before and taken the time to put in rollers and sit underneath a dryer. Well, I washed and feverishly blew my hair dry this morning. Ugh. If this were before no-buy month, I would have been at the salon, getting my hair done professionally. It would have been perfectly shiny and bouncy. *Focus, Natalie. Focus.* My hair would have looked great but my poor little bank account would have been anemic. Yes, that's more like it.

I drove down to the studio at the University of Miami (I didn't have to dig around my car for toll money, since I'm not spending money at the vending machine at work). The hosts, Toni and JR, were really sweet. When I saw the video posted online later, I noticed that the back of my hair fanned out! Gah. The thickness took over and it was all puffed out. Meh! My hair has zero discipline and I'm *not* good with a blow-dryer. I need some better products. I need to learn to take my time. *What were you thinking, Natalie?*

As for my nails, well, I took off the polish on my fingers because it was chipped. Their shape is holding up pretty well. I will just have naked nails. I'm not up for polishing them and messing it up. I don't trust my mani skills just yet. Plus, I have a decent nail bed. There's nothing wrong with naked nails. Now, as for my feet, the color is there but you can see where it's grown out a bit. If push comes to shove, I'll stop wearing my toes out. Peep toes aren't everything. Well, they are. Just not this month.

I emailed the link from the web show to the Youngster and he just was like, "Your hair is red?" Okay, so the lights on the set were pretty bright. And yes, my hair has an awful, harsh tint on it. My hairstylist doesn't speak English very well, so our communication about what color I want isn't great. So yes, I am paying for color that makes me look like Ronald McDonald when the lights hit it. But seriously, the Youngster didn't have to point that out. He didn't say much else about the spot, but I was happy with it.

Later he sent me a link to post on the blog. Maybe he sensed I was mini-vexed at his comment? I've been in enough relationships to know when things are going well and when it's time to reassess. The last thing I want to do is stay around too long.

It's been a long month and it's only halfway through.

FEBRUARY 14

I am pissed. I acted like a fool with the Youngster. He didn't pick up the phone and call for Valentine's Day. HE INSTANT MES-SAGED. No flowers. Nothing. I told him he didn't have to, because of no-buy month and all. But did I mean it? Obviously not! What's the matter with men? He should have known better. This is the guy who sent me flowers BEFORE we started dating. Between not going to NOLA and the lack of communication, it's looking spotty. It's not going well and I think both of us are getting tired.

FEBRUARY 16

My college friend Brian bought me lunch today and treated me to an arts festival in Coconut Grove. I told him about the Youngster.

His take? "Leave the kid alone." So Brian of him. If only it were that easy!! I enjoyed our friend date, though. Company is always good. I told some of my friends about the outing. They accused me of skirt-ing around my no-buy month. I mean, so be it if I have friends who are willing to buy me lunch every so often. Jeez. Who am I to deny them the pleasure of my company? Zora Neale Hurston lives!

FEBRUARY 19

It's over. Operation Natalie the Cougar is a wrap. The Youngster and I are over. I now dub him Man X. I was pissed off about the New Orleans trip. I thought about the times he had visited my home and the ex-girlfriend had called his phone. I blocked out a few things when we dated, but now that I'm acting all focused, cooking, not shopping, being a big girl, I am seeing things more clearly. On his New Orleans trip he expressed to one of our mutual friends that I was acting out. You think?

Okay. I instant messaged him that we should call it a wrap. Not my favorite way to call it off, but considering he *IM'd* me a Happy Valentine's Day (seriously, who does that?), it seemed only fitting.

He called the next day and then told me that he can't be what I need and it's over. Um, didn't I already cover that? But like a sucker, I immediately started crying on the phone. Why did I cry when he said it was over, when *I* had already broken up with *him?*

Whatever the case, it was over, because it needed to be. He was nice, fun and easy to talk to (when I could get him on the phone). But I'm a bit long in the tooth for something that's not going to lead anywhere. I will *not* waste my ovaries!

I am not happy. I am hurt. I feel hoodwinked, bamboozled and led astray. He met my mother. And she *liked him!* I liked him! Ugh! I hate it when shit doesn't work out. I hate starting over. What the hell just happened?

I so want to go shopping. Now. But I can't because of this no-buy month challenge. Nothing like having the eyes of blog readers and friends everywhere watching my every dime and move. I want to go visit my brother and my little niece in Nashville, but I can't buy a plane ticket. I can't even go out to a cheesy movie to distract my-self, or order in my favorite comfort food. I can't do anything to heal my wounds! How the hell am I going to stick to this no-buy month through this breakup? They don't call it retail therapy for nothing! What am I going to do?

My coworker/desk mate/work wife Julia had the nerve to say that I made the relationship all about me! What the hell? Aren't we ladies meant to stick together during times like these?! Did she just take *his* side? If we didn't have an arrangement of rotating cooking and bringing in lunch for each other during no-buy month, she and I would have exchanged some really nasty words. But she got me hooked on her couscous dishes, so I will behave. The things I must do to save a buck (and to cut down on preparing lunches)!

Man X bought a ticket for me to visit him in New York for my birthday on February 23 and now I won't be going. My birthday is screwed. Where can I celebrate a birthday...FOR FREE?

FEBRUARY 20

I blogged about needing a no-cost place to go for my birthday. Man X read it (he's still reading my blog?!) and emailed that I could use the ticket because he bought it for me. Damage control? Decency? That was nice of him. I am glad he offered, and happy that my birthday is back on. Still, a part of me is sad because it solidifies the fact that we are over. I. HATE. BREAKUPS.

My childhood friend Carly lives in New York, and she said I can hang with her and crash at her place. Amen for friends. Plus, I have a lot of friends in NYC. One of the good things about being a party girl is that you rack up some cool people in nice cities to hang with.

Can I do the Big Apple without spending any money? Can I avoid the temptations of clubs, cabs and alcohol?

FEBRUARY 22

I'm in New York! It's one of my favorite cities. I thought I'd be sharing it with the Youngster, er, Man X, but I am trying my best not to let the breakup ruin my weekend. Carly met me at the airport and we took the bus (only $2, much cheaper than a $20 shuttle) to her apartment in Harlem.

Tonight Carly and I went to the Museum of Modern Art. It's free Friday evenings. Normally when I visit New York, Carly and I are at happy hours. Now we indulged in fine art. Who knew doing things for free could be so classy? I'm determined to make the best of this weekend, given the circumstances.

FEBRUARY 23

Happy birthday to me! Happy birthday to me!

For some odd reason, I got the urge to go play in the snow.

How crazy is that? I turned a year older and I started acting younger. Plus, it's not like Miami ever gets snow, and I always schedule my visits home to Chicago when there's no snow on the ground. I wanted to clear my head a bit and figured walking over to Central Park could help. I misted up a bit, walking on the New York streets. I'm old enough to know not to stick around too long in a relationship that's not working, but a breakup—during your birthday, while you are not allowed to spend any extra cash—is a lot to handle.

On our way to the park, I ranted to Carly: "I should have never agreed to a long-distance relationship and I should have never dated someone that much younger than me. I shouldn't have fallen for the 'think long term' line that Man X fed me. People tell you anything to get your attention. I got too emotionally invested way too soon. I should have never let him meet my mother!" Hot tears fell on my cool skin as we traveled the city blocks. Carly insisted that everything was going to be OK with me and that sometimes shit just happens. I hope she's right. I've known her since preschool, so we've gotten each other through more than a few breakups over the years.

Luckily, reaching Central Park was a good distraction. I think I made about 5 snowballs, which I just tossed at no one and nothing in particular. Carly was a good sport, indulging in my newfound immaturity and taking photos of me with snowballs in my hand. After our playdate, I felt a little better.

Later on that night at Carly's apartment, it was like a big college reunion. My two friends from college came over to Carly's apartment and we drank all of Carly's Trader Joe's wine. They cheered me up about the breakup. One of my friends tried to cheer me up by reminding me that long-distance relationships are not Frugalista at all. That's right. If it's not frugal, I'm not doing it this month! Love life included.

After the wine fest, we hopped on the train and hit up a party that was free before midnight. We met some more of our friends there. Being with friends who have known me since college helped take my mind off my "situation." I am thankful to have friends who like to hang with me and have my back when times get tough...and

---

weird. I thought I'd be spending my birthday differently, but New York is a great city and my friends know how to have a good time. I am enjoying my moment as much as I can. No one wants to be around a wet blanket.

Man X didn't call but wished me happy birthday on Facebook. He didn't ask to see me, yet he knew I was just a few blocks away. Wow. Just a few weeks ago he would *fly* to see me, but now that I'm in the neighborhood, we don't see each other at all! It must really be over.

As much as I knew it was over when I came here, this just makes it all the more real…and painful.

FEBRUARY 24

I took the bus (only $2!) to LaGuardia Airport. My birthday was awesome, even though I had a few boo-hoo moments. I'm sure Carly has earned her wings for putting up with my drama.

When I first started my blog, I called up my friend Tanya to see if she could help me get some press. Tanya's a member of my journalists' association, the same one I've been in (off and on) since high school. I just found out that she booked me on CNN on Monday! CNN is major! The people at work gave me the approval to go on air. I was worried that they would try to stop me, saying I needed to focus on my "local news job." So far, so good. I'm loving work these days!

FEBRUARY 25

I was on CNN today. Yay! Gerri Willis, the host, was really cool. She's a major player in the personal finance/business reporting realm. The producer said I did a good job on air and everyone back at the office watched. It's nice to be noticed!

This blog thing is kind of fascinating. I'm reaching more people by writing less than 300 words per post than I could writing a 1,000 word story…and my blog isn't even edited. It's online and it's free, so whoever wants to read it can.

I called up Tanya to thank her and made a mental note that I got to keep it moving. It feels like there's momentum here!

FEBRUARY 26

Erykah Badu's new album dropped today. But could I buy it? NOOOOOOOOOOOOOOOOOOOOO. All because I wanted to be creative and do this no-buy month thing.

I am such a Baduist, it's not funny. *Mama's Gun?* Classic. I saw Erykah Badu in concert last summer and have only those memories to go on. I log on to her MySpace page, but it's not enough. I love to muse over my music, experience it, not point and click a few samples. Speaking of music, the CD player in my Honda doesn't work. My Kanye West, Common and who all else's albums got gobbled up in that stupid CD player. My life has been one of snapping fingers, getting low and shawty you a 10 from listening to the radio.

I think I am unraveling a bit. I like the way my bank account looks, but I don't think it's too much to ask to be able to buy new music. February is the shortest month of the year, but it's feeling pretty long.

FEBRUARY 28

Total amount not spent in February: $384.03. Here's the breakdown of what I saved:

> *$41.03 on electricity (Now that I sleep with the lights off.)*
>
> *$213 on food (I figured that's the minimum I spent in restos each month. Instead of eating out, I ate at home and took my lunch to work, and occasionally someone took pity and bought me a meal.)*

$70 on hair (I'm doing it myself. Not happy about it.)

$40 on nails (Natural is the new polished?)

$20 on a car wash (No way was I gonna wash it myself. I drove it filthy.)

That's a grand total of $384.03 NOT spent!!!!!!!!!! This no-buy stuff really works.

CHAPTER 3

March

DEBTS

xxxxxxxxxxxxxxxxxxxxxxxxxxxxxxxxxxxxxxx

CREDIT CARDS: $9,353.87

CAR LOAN: $8,040.36

STUDENT LOAN: $2,538.18

xxxxxxxxxxxxxxxxxxxxxxxxxxxxxxxxxxxxxxx

TOTAL DEBTS: $ 19,932.41

xxxxxxxxxxxxxxxxxxxxxxxxxxxxxxxxxxxxxxx

MARCH 1

I did it. I did it. I DID IT! I didn't buy one unnecessary thing during the month of February! Whooooo-wheee! I saved nearly $400. I am a woman. I am a woman who can save money. *Work it, Nat!*

 I think I can. I think I can. Who knew I could actually save almost FOUR HUNDRED DOLLARS IN ONE MONTH? I've been doing this all wrong. Like ALL wrong. For years. Well, eyes have been opened. It's all about to change.

Cheering fest aside, I am a little nervous. I have to keep this thing going and I don't think it will be easy. The editors at work wanted me to quit blogging after February but I pitched an outright hissy to keep it going. I stormed Boss Lady's office. (I'm sure foaming at the mouth was not attractive.) I bitched to every reporter in the office. And trust me, they have big ears and mouths. I bought up a bunch of domains on GoDaddy.com just in case my blog got the boot. Frugalista ain't going down without a fight. Free Frugalista!

The Frugalista Files has been on CNN, and now the *Miami Herald* wants to cut it? I should be at the table on this one. No more decisions made about me in closed-door meetings. I SHOULD BE AT THE TABLE. My blog was hot. I won't be denied. I won't! I DESERVE this.

I ain't no punk. I, for darn sure, wasn't going down quietly. Maybe my boss had mercy on my soul. Maybe she wanted peace in the Everglades. Maybe she was worried more about what would happen if I didn't get my way. After 7 years as an employee I was past due to get what I wanted for once. What I REALLY wanted.

Boss Lady made some calls, had some meetings and worked it out. I had a meeting with the business editor and multimedia editor to plead my case, after Boss Lady greased the corporate wheels.

Long story short: I can keep my blog going on a trial basis. Under the "Keep Natalie Quiet" agreement (okay, it wasn't called that, but it sure felt like it), I won't be getting any more pay for the blog. All good. My blog about the money isn't all about the money. It's about me.

Noted Boss Lady after the victory: "You never asked my approval in the first place and you dragged me into this!"

Oops. Did I do that? (*Bats eyelashes.*)

"Take this blog thing as far as it can go," Boss Lady said.

Yeayahh! My antics worked.

It's hard out here for a reporter. I know I'm going to have to be on my best behavior at work. I don't think I have any favors left. No more foaming at the mouth. Maybe I'll just bare my teeth as needed. Time to stop not getting what I want out of my job. This blog, well, it makes me happy. Period. It's been a while since I've been happy at the desk job. Let's keep it going.

Last night I helped my friend Marika pack up her apartment because she's moving. I had on the glamour girl makeup from my second CNN appearance (yep, twice they wanted me), so I needed to get out of the house. Even if just to pack boxes. I like looking like a Miami Heat Dancer—minus the hot pants and size 2 frame. Heh.

Still brooding over the breakup with the Youngster, er, Man X, so gotta stay busy. When you get to be my age, you probably have a few breakups under your belt. So why don't they get easier instead of harder? Seems like they're easier when it's something dramatic, like a dude stealing money from your bank account or dating your best friend. A breakup just because the relationship didn't work is harder. I am getting pretty tired of them.

Marika is moving to a more affordable place, just a few streets down from where she lives. Her new place is gorgeous, with a better view. Who knew? So many condo rental deals to be had these days with the shady real estate down here. I still couldn't afford her rent, though. She's an attorney.

She had a pair of never-worn wedge sandals that she let me have. Yay! They are super cute and never fit her feet right. One woman's trash is another woman's treasure. And a girl can always use a sandal in Miami. Frugalista tip: Friends often have similar taste. Shake 'em down when they are moving and vulnerable.☺

MARCH 4

I'm under the weather. I got this cough/sniffle thing that's going around. Feeling a little bit better and won't go to the doctor. My health insurance has a yearly $250 deductible, so any trips to the doc would be out of pocket. (And I still owe $48 from a previous doctor's visit.) It's just a cold. Orange juice is my doctor now.

But something else is bothering me. This thing has been

weighing on me for longer than I care to remember, but now I'm getting more emails and calls about it and my "put a positive spin on it" technique isn't cutting it anymore. I have to deal with it full on.

My good college friend Cliff is dying. It sucks. It sucks writing this. I know he hasn't been well for years, even though he never talked about what was wrong. Every year I noticed changes. First the seizures. Then he couldn't drive anymore. The surgical scars on his head that he often covered with a cap. The exercises with flash cards he casually mentioned he had to do. Last year I helped him pick out some blazers online to buy for the journalism convention we all were going to. He backed out at the last minute and ended up moving to Kansas City to live with his mother shortly thereafter. He was looking forward to the convention and seeing everyone, but just didn't have the strength to go.

He has brain cancer. He never told me.

I have tried to visit him since January, but he's thwarted my attempts and other friends' attempts to see him. It's hard dealing with a life-threatening illness. It's also hard to be a friend of someone who's dealing with a life-threatening illness.

Finally, Cliff is at peace with what is happening to him. He has reached the point where he is open to seeing people. So now I am going. The airline ticket is $338. The car rental is $66. I am going to use the $35 left over from my canceled New Orleans trip on the ticket.

I called him to check in, to see how he's doing. But it's past the calling stage. Shit.

Everyone has been asking what I'm going to do with the money I saved. I am using it to buy a plane ticket to visit my friend Cliff, who has about 2 weeks to live. His friend Bryant put me in touch with his family, who, thankfully, has given me the okay to see Cliff. Our mutual friend John can go, too. His mother made it clear that we better come sooner than later.

MARCH 6

One of the many things I learned from no-buy month is that I have enough. If I had the opportunity to do TV appearances before the no-buy month, I most certainly would have spent about $200 buying new shirts for the "right look." But because of the no-buy month, I just closet shopped and found clothes that were just fine. They were more than fine. They were perfect.

Before the no-buy month, I felt that I needed to buy things just to "get it right." When it came time for hair appointments, I thought I needed a professional's touch to feel good about the way my hair looked. Don't get me wrong. There's nothing like a professional styling, but the question I have learned to ask myself is, "Do I need it or do I want it?" Having my hair done was a $70 to $105 monthly want. That's too much for me to spend at this stage in my life.

I have many talents and an aptitude for learning. Perfecting the arch of my eyebrows or styling my hair is something I can teach myself. I refuse to not look good. But I also refuse to pay too much to look good. Frugalista tip: Before you shell out the cash, ask yourself if this is something you really *need* or just something you *want*. You'd be surprised!

MARCH 7

I'm renewed in my quest to become an outright Frugalista.

Several people in the office and several readers have commented that they don't carry a credit card balance. Living life with *no* balance? Regular working people who found a way not to have debt? I mean, if their interest rate shot up to 30 percent, it wouldn't matter. They would be paying 30 percent interest on zero—nothing!

I had an "aha" moment. My salary won't allow me to pay off this debt in a year, but I am going to keep on the frugal track and slay at least one of my credit cards by next year. I could slay the other one by the middle of the following year. Slow and steady is how I'm going to have to pay down this debt—and I will pay it down.

MARCH 8

My former coworker Juan got married today to another former coworker. Newsrooms are breeding grounds for love! I'm so excited.

Initially, I told Juan that I was bringing a date, thinking that Man X would be in town for it. Due to my, ahem, recent change in relationship status, I invited Vivian to attend so I would have someone to talk to, and she was thrilled. She's one of those people who loves a good wedding. (Well, she enjoys any reason to dress up and eat good food. At the end of the day, a wedding is just a big party.)

I wore a light blue silk halter dress with a chocolate Pucci-like design that I had bought the previous year but had never worn. Since I've stopped eating out so much, I've lost a few pounds, so my clothes are fitting perfectly these days. I'm so glad I was able to wear the dress. And the colors matched the wedding colors, so I was even more thrilled about that. Just call me the wedding guest mascot!

My shoes were some peep-toe pumps that showed only part of my big toe. I didn't want to go out and get a pedicure. And guess what? No one noticed that my toenails weren't freshly painted. Viva la Frugalista!

I bought the happy couple a gift for $60 from the wedding registry at Macy's. I couldn't really find a more affordable gift on the registry. I made a mental note to start a gift fund for weddings, births and birthdays.

Juan's wedding was at a gorgeous church in Coral Gables, one of the toniest parts of Miami-Dade County. The reception had an open bar (yippee) and sit-down dinner. I know this wedding wasn't cheap. If I were to get married, I think the wedding would have to be at the courthouse, given my budget.

At the dinner, I sat at a table with several former coworkers, many of whom got better jobs at the other papers in South Florida, like the *Palm Beach Post* and the *SunSentinel*. It was like a mini-reunion. Kelvin, who used to work in my office but now works in Palm Beach, told me that he saw me on CNN! "I looked up from my desk and there you were on television," Kelvin said. "I want to be a Frugalista!"

Heehee! Join the party, Kelv! Men are welcome!

MARCH 9

I'm sick. Did I party too hard at the wedding? It's not easy to be a sick Frugalista. I am still sniffly and have been guzzling small bottles of OJ all week, which set me back 8 bucks. Frugalista lesson learned: buy 1 half-gallon container for $3.50, instead of small bottles at about $1.50 apiece.

All I want is some soothing Thai or Chinese food…. I'm sick! I need to nurture myself! I caved and had lunch at my favorite Thai place once this week and Chinese takeout twice. Total: $21. Yikes. Being frugal is not the easiest.

When I entered the Thai restaurant, the owner treated me like an extra on that old show *Cheers*. "Natalieeee! Where have you been? I missed you." Yep, I'm sure his books are all off since I stopped going daily. I explained the no-buy month to him. He seemed *really* interested. Could a business owner be a Frugalist(o)? Hmmm.

MARCH 12

My journalism association asked me to serve on a panel tonight on educating the South Florida community on how to access the media. Every year we hold the free panel as a service to make sure everyone has a fair shake at getting their stories told in the media. This year we held the panel at a community center in the Liberty City neighborhood. I think every nonprofit worker and community leader this side of Interstate 95 showed up. I represented the *Miami Herald*, aka Ma Herald, on the panel. The other guests included editors and producers from the cable, television and radio media outlets in town. I told everyone about working as a news reporter and how we are always looking for stories. I told the crowd that they need not bother me or any journalist at 5 p.m., deadline time, if they want to be listened to.

After the end of the session, the panelists mingled with the 70 or so people in the audience. I had a few people ask me about my blog and some of the books on frugal living I had referenced on it.

I'm so used to people talking to me about how to get their pet projects in the press. It was kind of cool to talk to people about saving money!

It turned out that one of the panelists, Paula, is the calendar editor at the alternative newsweekly by day but runs her own beauty blog in her downtime. I had read her blog before—it's really popular—but I didn't know that she was in Miami! I'm starting to think that every woman under age 35 has a blog and a superpower name!

I made sure to chat Paula up. I enjoyed talking to the audience members, but no way was I going to let the evening end without talking to a major blogger. Paula and I decided to meet for lunch soon. Good times.

MARCH 18

Tax time! Fun! Last year I filed using Turbo Tax (TT), which was free because I was a first-time user. This year TT stuck me with a $30 bill. Meh. Well, time is money, as they say, and TT is much faster than the frustrating pencil-and-paper calculations I used to do.

I'll deduct that $30 from my $1,600 tax refund. If I didn't withhold so much money from my paycheck, I'd have more cash throughout the year. One year I actually had to pay more money at tax time and that was no fun. Also, I'm getting $600 from the economic stimulus plan. What to do with $2,200? Throw the cash at debts? Beef up my savings?

One thing's for sure, I have NO intention of "stimulating the economy" by shopping. Look at my credit card bills and bank statements; I've done my civic duty more than most Americans. You can't fool me, Mr. President.

MARCH 19

Good things come to those who wait! It's really, really true! Erykah Badu is giving a free Miami Beach concert on March 28.

MARCH 22/23

I arrived in Kansas City yesterday to visit my friend Cliff. Spent yesterday at the hospital and will probably head back there in a bit.

The flight and rental car for this trip cost me $404, but there is no price tag on telling a loved one how much he means to you. After doing the no-buy month in February, I had the extra money to pay for this trip in CASH. I never realized just how good that would feel.

I parked my car in remote, cheapo $3 parking at the Miami airport. It would have been cheaper to have a friend drop me off at the airport but my flight left at 6 a.m. on Friday. It would be a lot to ask someone to drive me there at the crack of dawn. Plus, I would have fumed if someone woke up late and made me miss my flight. I know my independent streak can be costly, but no way was I going to miss/delay this trip.

My friend John and I are splitting the hotel room. I met him through the journalists' association—it really is a cult, er, family. John's on the frugal plan, too. We take turns paying for meals. Fortunately, I get to pay for lunch, which is always cheaper than dinner.

Cliff recognized me at the hospital. He even let out a little laugh when John and I talked to him. As soon as we arrived in his room, the nurse's aide brushed his teeth and wiped his face. That's right. Get my boy right.

When I held his hand and tried to tell him how I felt about our friendship, I started crying. His mother patted me and told me not to cry. I tried to be strong. You're supposed to be upbeat and not make things worse when you visit someone dying in the hospital. But I couldn't help myself. I am not that strong. Strong people can hold it together in adversity. I just said that I loved him and then the waterworks came. I am not the one with terminal cancer. I'm such a wuss. But I said what I felt.

Cliff's entire family—his dad, two brothers and mom—are always by his side. His mom is so sweet. We got to talk about Cliff. She filled in some of the blanks that he never told me.

Basically, when he first fell ill years ago, the doctors told him to enjoy his life and have fun. Go on every trip he wanted to go on. Do everything he ever wanted to. Cliff was always traveling to basketball games and tournaments. He even came down to Florida on a trip with one of his brothers. I remember when I had all my friends in Washington, D.C., meet me for a margarita and Mexican food "brunch" after homecoming one year. I made sure Cliff could get a ride with one of our friends from Baltimore to attend. I was worried that he wouldn't make it but he did. I loved having him there, listening to his god-awful laugh, which I always found oddly comforting.

John took Cliff's brothers and me out for drinks and dinner. It's weird meeting someone's family members in person after hearing about them for so many years. His brother Brian mentioned how Cliff used to email him articles on parenting and he could never understand why. Heehee. I kept quiet during that one. Cliff had told me that his nephew used to bite kids at day care. I hope my family and friends never meet up when I'm not in the room!

When I got back to Miami, I felt drained but oddly content. I wasn't prepared for it. Cliff had never talked about the cancer. I never realized he was so sick. But then again, how can you prepare? You just have to live, right? I am so glad I got to see him. I know I did the right thing by going.

MARCH 30

Erykah Badu was awesome. Just awesome. Rapper Common and Talib Kweli also performed at the concert. The crowd was vibing. Chills down my spine. I took some pictures but the guard told me to put my camera away, so I couldn't take more. And it really was free. Like, free. Like, I paid nothing to get in the door. I didn't even buy a drink, although a guy bought my friend and me a drink. So cool.

MARCH 31

For the second time this year Marlon, an attorney whom I use as a source, has hit me up to trademark my blog. I don't know a thing about trademarks. It's $375. I have extra money now. I guess I should do it. I called my mother and she said go for it.

If I let him do my trademark, I can't use him as a source any-more (ethics of Journalism 101). Our relationship would have to be strictly attorney/client. I figure I've quoted him enough, anyway. And this Frugalista thing is interesting. It makes the crowd go wild. Rawr! Everyone wants a piece of me (I am being dramatic, I know). I'm going for it!

CHAPTER 4

April

DEBTS

xxxxxxxxxxxxxxxxxxxxxxxxxxxxxxxxxxxxx

CREDIT CARDS: $9,156.94

CAR LOAN: $7,758.79

STUDENT LOAN: $2,489.26

xxxxxxxxxxxxxxxxxxxxxxxxxxxxxxxxxxxxx

TOTAL DEBTS: $ 19,404.99

xxxxxxxxxxxxxxxxxxxxxxxxxxxxxxxxxxxxx

APRIL 1

This is no April Fools' joke. This month's challenge is to spend just $50 per week on vittles. Means more cooking at home. The grocery store is a place that remains a mystery to me. The problem is that I am just one person. I do not have bright-eyed little ones to cook for. It's just me. I do not feel right buying up a whole chicken. My grocery store sells ready-made meals and all you have to do is reheat them in the oven. It's kind of taking the easy (and a tad pricier) way out. Publix has ready-made fried chicken, too. I mean, it's cheaper than going to a restaurant.

I should just eat fruits and vegetables and leave this grocery shopping thing alone. I know I need to start cooking more, though, even if I just buy a smaller piece of chicken to cook for myself, as a happy medium. One thing is for sure: this month Natalie needs to master the kitchen.

APRIL 2

Did I mention that I live in an apartment that needs some work? There's a termite infestation in my apartment complex, so I have to pack up my groceries and some clothes and move out for 2 days while they fumigate (!) my place. I am going to have my neighbor Rob babysit my groceries because he lives in a different building in my complex—one that is not being fumigated. I can't have my chicken tasting like termite spray! Gag. Back in the day, I'd just check into a hotel, watch movies on demand and eat all my meals in restaurants. Those were the days.... Now I have to find a friend who will put up with me. I hate not being independent! But a $250 hotel will set me back majorly. I'm thinking Marika. I mean, I *did* help her pack up her old place when she was moving. I need to couch surf.

Frugalista hair report: Last weekend I did a home do. My hair is so friggin' thick. My wrists are already beat down from working on a computer all day as a hack, er, writer, and bumping and curling my hair isn't helping. But I have no plans to get my hair done, other than my relaxer and color rinse every 6 weeks (Frugalistas have to draw the line somewhere). Luckily, I have some shampoo around the house I can use. I went through my bathroom cabinet and realized I have so many products that I don't even use. To keep my hair looking good without spending salon money, I also bought some setting lotion that's supposed to let your hair dry out smoothly. I consider it a Frugalista investment.

I've been blow-drying my hair quickly because I'm too impatient for a roller set and that's not good. By the time I blast my ancient dryer on hot and high, there's a carpet of hair all over my bathroom. I am baking out my hair. Meh.

Today I roller set the do. I used the big old purple rollers I've had since college. I sectioned off my hair and tried to roll it like they do at the salon. Gah. I'm so out of practice. I didn't quite sit underneath my dryer, also from college, as long as I should have but long enough for a curl to take hold. My hair is puffier than at the salon, but it's presentable. Tried oiling it down so it looked shiny. A shiny puff ball is better than a dull one. I wrapped my hair underneath my scarf, so it would lie down a little more. In time I'll get the hang of it. In time.

APRIL 4

Thank goodness for Marika! I'll be staying with her for 2 nights while they nuke those 'mites. I'll buy her some food while I'm there as a thank-you. I am not the most comfortable in my own kitchen, so I'm not taking over the kitchen at her place. I'll have to eat out and pick up ready-made food. Things are going to be tight this week. I ate up most of the food in my refrigerator in anticipation of the move.

I want to do something nice for Marika to thank her for letting me couch surf. I could make dinner, but she's a really good cook. I'm not convinced she would trust me in her kitchen. (I'm not sure I would trust me in her kitchen.) Several readers suggested buying her dinner, which is doable. I'm not so sure I will make my $50 food budget this week, either. I spent nearly $16 on food yesterday—the Thai place brought me down. I had dinner there, too. I couldn't resist. Gah!

APRIL 7

Homelessness never felt so sweet. Marika's building is hot: bay view, valet parking, elevator operator, the whole bit. We didn't get to hang out, because she's working long hours, but I am happy to have a friend who a) lets me stay with her for 2 nights and b) lives well.

Am I envious? No. Seeing someone else's success motivates me to work harder and be smarter about my money. Also, for all my bellyaching, I have no reason to complain about my life. It's a great one.

Now, I don't play "keep up with the Joneses" with friends, but I do read glossy magazines. I love my *Glamour* magazine. And it loves me. You see a new look or a new hairstyle and you want to imitate it. These days I'm just reading it for informational purposes and not inspirational. I'm taking a break from the shopping game. Plus, some of the hair tips aren't so bad. A new barrette is cheaper to buy than a new wardrobe.

While Marika worked and I waited for her to get home, I went to the mall.... Okay, I know, I know...but where do stranded women go? The mall. While there, I saw an adorable blouse for like $16. I felt a little bit guilty, but it was cute and I deserved a gold star for my hard work. Plus, I needed to pass the time away. Just because I'm temporarily homeless doesn't mean I need to start hanging out at libraries! I bought it and bought dinner for Marika. Not so bad, right?

APRIL 8

It's funny—now that I've been doing this Frugalista thing for a couple of months, I can see how it's changed some of my relationships.

I have different sets of friends. One set travels to hip cities for events such as jazz concerts, taste festivals and all-star games. I love them, but this Frugalista can't keep up. They always ask me to go with them and I always tell them no because the trips are pricey. I hate feeling like the odd woman out, but I am responsible for my fiscal health. If I can't swing it, I can't swing it.

When I started cutting back on expenses, I tried to get all my friends on the Frugalista bandwagon. I wish I could say I asked them to join because I wanted them to prosper financially, but really that wasn't the case. I just knew that if I had a no-spend circle around me, I wouldn't be tempted to burn cash the way I used to!

My friends here in Florida are sweet girls, but much of our

friendship is based on kicking it. I hate always being the grouch who says no. I'm sure they think that I am a party pooper or I am making excuses. They considered me frugal LONG before I started this blogging thing just because I don't travel as much as they do. Isn't that weird? They go to Cancún every year to party, while Nat can't go. I guess frugality is all relative. I live beyond my means but I don't cross international boundaries doing it. I party stateside, at least.☺

Sometimes I feel like the resident miser by repeatedly saying no, no, no. Some people think that because you are a "professional," you are supposed to be able to spend money and do all the hot shit. Well, once upon a time, I did do the hot shit. The problem is that I kicked it too much. Look at my account balances! Hotels are costly. I'm starting to realize, even if I can get a room for $150 by splitting with them, that's $150 that I should not be adding to my debt. What's the point of going on a vacation when you have to run it on a credit card or you have to nibble from your weak savings account?

Every Sunday we used to head down to South Beach and kick it for the entire day. Parking, drinking, eating…it all adds up. And, you start seeing the same people again and again. I am aging out of the system. I'd like to see some fresh meat. Not the same guys. And I'm sure the same guys are tired of seeing me. Plus it's time away from getting my work done. I truly enjoyed it, but where does it get you? I can't keep this fly and broke routine up.

I worried that my mom would be a little bit embarrassed about her daughter complaining about her bills (online, to the world!), but she has really been on board with the Frugalista program. Maybe she's happy to see me excited about something. Or maybe she believes in the project. She's retired and the house is paid off. She basically admitted to me that she's coasting. She doesn't shop like she used to. And she doesn't get her hair done like she used to when my parents were married. I guess the divorce, which was costly and long, got her on the Frugalista plan and I didn't even notice. I see it now. I know she wanted her dream car instead of the used Honda, but she doesn't complain. She's riding out in her Honda Accord that's paid off and seems to be doing okay. I'm jealous!☺

My brother hasn't said too much about the whole thing. He, especially, is just happy that I got on TV. He's such a guy. He doesn't sweat the details.

And then there're the friends who are most honest with you. My best friend, Erika, doesn't think that my salary at the paper is all that low. She says I've been reckless with the cash. *Ouch.* I still say it's both. I could always use $5,000 more a year.

APRIL 9

Was I complaining about money? Well, things are looking up. I did a freelance article for TheRoot.com, which is owned by the Washington Post Company, about taking a "vow of frugality" to stop my promiscuous spending. They are paying me $200! A college friend is an editor there and asked me to do the piece. I put the link to my blog in the article and now my traffic is crazy. The Washington Post Company also has a relationship with Slate.com, so my article made the home page of *Slate*. Yeah! Why do I need print again? Internet pimpin' forever!

APRIL 10

Damn! Work is weird. Buyout offers were sent by email (email!) to some of my coworkers. The newspaper business is so shaky these days with circulation down and advertising soft. Cut. Cut. Cut. Two percent of the *Herald's* full-time workforce is being cut. Some employees have been asked to "volunteer" to leave. If they don't, then there will be layoffs.

I have a bad feeling in my stomach.

Those who received emails were crying. Just because you are eligible doesn't mean that you will necessarily get cut…. It means you could get cut, depending on who decides to leave the paper on their own or how senior you are. It was gruesome to watch the Big Boss stop by some desks and walk employees into her big glass office with the blinds drawn. All I could think about was how I really need to get my finances in order. The only good thing about buyouts/ layoffs at the paper is that you're given a settlement package, at least 8 weeks of salary as a severance. The bad thing about buyouts is that you're unemployed. That's the one worst thing buyouts and getting let go have in common.

Getting a job in journalism is no walk in the park these days. I still have a job. I need to make it work for me. That means finding a way to save up 6 months of living expenses and eliminating debt. I won't be staging any more revolutions in the office. Now is not the time. *Stay low, Natalie, and keep moving. Stay low.*

APRIL 11

Okay, so I filled out the questionnaire on a dating site. I've never dated online before. The site sure did ask a lot of questions. I wonder if getting government clearance for a federal job is as thorough?! Gracious!

I guess I did all right. I got accepted. (I sound like a high school senior who got into her top college choice.) Anyway, a few of my friends have mentioned that it's a good site to meet quality guys. I scrolled around to read about some of the people that the site suggested may be a good match. The site sent me a guy with potential: Malcolm. He's 39 and over 6 feet. He says he likes traveling and dining out. Friends describe him as honest, affectionate and conservative. Hmmm. Conservative? I like to have a good time.

The cost to meet Malcolm and others of his ilk: $59.95 per month. Oh, hell no! I don't need a love that bad. I will not pay more than I pay for my student loan looking for love. I'm trying to get rid of my bills, not add to them.

Mr. Right and I will have to meet at a club or a grocery store or through a family introduction, with no finder's fee attached!

APRIL 12

Had dinner with Cliff's friend Bryant last night, who was in town visiting his family. Bryant has helped me get the 411 on Cliff's condition and this was our first time hanging out after many, many phone calls and emails. Haven't had a chance to catch up with him much since last month. We both know Cliff isn't doing well. Cliff's mom mentioned he was "gravely" ill…. In our conversations Bryant and I both just say Cliff's not doing well. We haven't yet mentioned to each other that he will probably die soon. It's too painful to say the one thing we're both thinking.

Bryant suggested dinner, which meant $$, and I was not sure if this was a date or friendly hanging out. Or was it a little bit of both? Was he going to pay for it? I can never tell. I had my debit card on hand, but this little Frugalista doesn't have money for expensive meals these days. Downtown Fort Lauderdale isn't known for affordable dining. And Fort Lauderdale gives out parking tickets as a sport! Luckily, as soon as we met up in Fort Lauderdale, Bryant said he was going to pay for everything because he knows I'm doing the saving money/Frugalista thing. I was relieved and then worried…. Will men now see me as needy? A woman who needs to be cared for? That's not good. Am I a liability to a man's wallet? I can carry my own…kind of.

Anyway, the food was great. We talked about Cliff. We talked about this journalism thing. Bryant's still hanging out at the *Baltimore Sun*. He's down with the print thing, but I'm worried print media will be a thing of the past in the near future. Bryant is sweet. From an unfortunate circumstance, I have made a new friend. I am thankful for that. I wonder what Cliff would think about Bryant and me hanging out? Bless him.

APRIL 13

My blog was mentioned in the Holy Grail of newspapers! The *New York Times!* That TheRoot.com article was the BEST EVER!! I keep reading and rereading what Dan Mitchell wrote about me:

> *"Once upon a time," writes Natalie P. McNeal, "I was financially promiscuous, giving up my cash to any peep-toe pump, nail salon or hairdresser on the block." At TheRoot.com, Ms.*

McNeal, a Miami Herald *reporter, describes how she took a vow of frugality in February. She has become, she says, "a financially chaste, respectable woman." In February, "I saved nearly $400," she says. "In March, I saved about $200." Her tale, told in real time, can be found on her blog, The Frugalista Files. Here, her message of frugality takes on an evangelistic flavor, with only a smidge of irony. "The life of a frugal," she writes, "can be considered a righteous one."*

Now that's HUGE! Maybe I don't suck as a journalist. Take that! Take that! (said in P. Diddy's voice). The really cool part is that the traffic on my blog is going up. Frugalista takeover. So maybe paying for my new skills has "paid off." Well, maybe paid off in recognition. Frugalista capitalism! Freelance for your hustle.

Now, if I can keep freelancing and riding out this blog thing, I may be able to speed up paying off debts. It's like a twofer: freelance money and blog recognition.

I showed the article to my coworker/work wife, Julia. "I haven't seen you write like this for the *Miami Herald*," she said. It was her way of saying she liked it, but OUCH! I mean, covering city commission meetings and local news isn't the most creative outlet.

April 14

Got my tax refund! One thousand immediately went to pay off credit card debt. I am feeling really smart. My credit card debt is lower now and I'm on track. I am a fabulous Frugalista! ☺ Some good things, some bad.

The good ☺ is:

I made a $1,000 dent in that credit card bill.

My electricity bill was $107.50 in January, $66.47 in February and $62.09 in March. Wow, look what happens when you learn to sleep with the lights off!

My cell phone bill was $76.78. The month before: $85.83. (I get a $40 allowance from the company, too!) I stopped calling all my friends while driving in my car like an overgrown teenager. I always run out of daytime minutes because of it.

The bad ☹ is:

So much for spending just $50 a week on food. This month I spent:

$5.25 Chinese food lunch

$7.48 Thai dinner

$10.55 Cuban lunch (shrimp creole)

$5.57 Chinese takeout

$8.43 Thai lunch

$14.98 Publix run

$17 Atlantic Bar & Grill (I took a new coworker out for drinks. She had bought dinner.)

$11.15 Publix run

$14.93 Dinner at Pasha's (when I was homeless and staying with Marika)

$25.14 Dinner at Pasha's (I bought my friend the meal as a repayment.)

$7.37 Cuban lunch

$4.19 Chicken lunch special at my Peruvian chicken takeout spot

$15 Lunch at Starbucks

$15 Three different pizza runs

The not so bad is:

Transportation. This month I spent:

$20 on gas

Clothing. This month I spent:

$16.04 Arden B. blouse (I wore it on a dinner date Friday.)

$20.30 Banana Republic dress (I've worn it to work.)

$20.30 Banana Republic dress (I bought the same dress as a birthday gift for a friend because I loved it so much.)

So I spent about $162 on food, mostly from eating out. Oink. Fashionwise, I still think I did great. Less than $60 and I got 2 dresses and a blouse. Holla! I gave in and went shopping because, well, I could. I had deprived myself for much of February and March. I wanted a treat. I wanted to feel a bit more normal. I was a little hesitant. I called a friend before I made the purchases and got it "approved." I can't do this Frugalista thing alone!

APRIL 15

More good news! I got a friend request on Facebook from a real-life author who read about me in the *New York Times*. It was just a mention but people really do read every article in that newspaper. The woman, Alexis Claiborne, wrote a popular novel and even sold the screen rights. And she wants to be my friend. On Facebook! She said she's coming to Miami in a few weeks to finish up another novel she's writing.

Clearly, a writer's life is different than my life. I always considered myself more of a journalist than a writer. Daily hack may be more like it. Newsroom sweatshop worker would be a good description, too. Not a writer for real. Like, a "has been on book tours" writer. Like, a "has an agent" writer. Like, a "can come to Miami Beach to finish up a novel because she doesn't have to report to a desk job" writer. She said she liked my "vow of frugality" article. I ran out and got her book (okay, I admit, I hadn't read it). It was $6 on sale at Barnes & Noble. Viva la Frugalista! I'm going to check her out when she comes to town.

APRIL 16

I wrote about buying the $16 Arden B. blouse on my blog and then heard from a lot of readers who were aghast that I made a purchase. Some said I was backsliding to my old shop-and-spend habits. Others said I deserved it and it was a good buy.

I say I deserved the darn blouse. I was alone and was hanging out at the mall when I was homeless. Marika wasn't home and I didn't really want to be in her place when she wasn't there. Also, I've spent $16 on worse things. It's not like I was an alcoholic going to the bar…is it?

I'm sorry, clothing makes me feel good. I just know now that I can't buy much else, or the chants of my readers will be in my ears. I feel like I now have a little devil on one shoulder and an angel on the other. *Do it. Don't do it. Do it. Don't do it.* When did buying clothing become an evil thing? Gah! I need to think about this more. I don't want to turn into a miser, but I know that now is not the time to backslide. When you are out of prison, you don't get thrown on the street. You get sent to transitional housing. I need that. There needs to be a halfway house for debtors.

I have to find a way to trust myself and what I'm doing.

APRIL 18

The National Association of Black Journalists holds its convention in July in a different city every year. I missed early bird registration, so I must pay $375, which is $50 more. A flight to the host city, Chi-Town, will be at least $300. I have a place to stay while there—Hotel de Mama's House—so I don't have to spring for a hotel. The convention is for professional enrichment. There are workshops, parties, er, networking opportunities and guest speakers. My company is giving me $100 toward costs. I put in to work overtime during Memorial Day weekend, so that extra money will help with costs. Yay! Planning ahead, for a change.

APRIL 19

Chrystia Freeland of the *Financial Times,* a *major* London-based business newspaper, wrote about my blog. Am I becoming the poster child for frugality? She made fun of me for posting about Dunkin' Donuts offering free doughnuts. I mean, I love posting on free things people can get. I am the Frugalista fairy. My readers are emailing me all the time about free events, food or drinks. There are plenty of companies that like to give away freebies, just to get people in their stores. Who am I not to share the information?

She seemed shocked that an American girl would cut her spending. Yikes. So people overseas think that all Americans do is spend and waste? That's not good. We'll have to change that.

This Frugalista thing is something.

APRIL 24

I went on National Public Radio's *Talk of the Nation* to talk about being a Frugalista. The producer there read my "vow of frugality" article on TheRoot.com and loved it. Said she wanted to have me on because I wasn't like most frugal people, "who don't eat meat." Liked that I'm just a regular girl trying to pay her bills.

Public radio is revered by everyone—even my bosses. They were pleased with the CNN stuff, but NPR and its premier talk show, well, now that's really something. One of my coworkers, Robert, told me that he wouldn't be surprised to see me on a commercial hawking the frugality of fast food. What is he talking about?

On NPR I got a call from a guy who said he's gaining more weight by cooking at home. (He's just eating too much of his own food. I know the feeling.) I also know a lot of people who say that eating healthy is more expensive. Take a browse around Whole Foods or The Fresh Market and you may not see the same prices as, say, oh, at a big-box grocery store. Personally, my meals are rather basic: meat, grain and a vegetable. Complicated dishes sound great but would take a lot of grocery time and I'm a baby when it comes to cooking. I'm not breaking the bank for exotic ingredients in a dish I may hate.

I buy frozen salmon, shrimp and tilapia in bulk from a discount warehouse. The salmon and tilapia steaks are already divided up. I can just take out 1 or 2 and they thaw quickly. They're easy to bake and it takes just 15 minutes. While the fish is cooking, I toss some broccoli in a microwavable plastic bag, add a bit of butter and microwave the whole thing for a few minutes. I'm cool with the simple meals. I season the fish different ways. Sometimes it's just garlic salt and cayenne pepper; other times I use jerk seasoning. And I make just enough for 1 meal when I make something I love, like spaghetti, or I wind up eating way more than I should.

Natalie McNeal giving cooking advice? What is going on?

CHAPTER 5

May

```
DEBTS

xxxxxxxxxxxxxxxxxxxxxxxxxxxxxxxxxxxxx

CREDIT CARDS:   $8,160.04

CAR LOAN:       $7,476.05

STUDENT LOAN:  $2,440.28


xxxxxxxxxxxxxxxxxxxxxxxxxxxxxxxxxxxxx

TOTAL DEBTS:   $18,076.37

xxxxxxxxxxxxxxxxxxxxxxxxxxxxxxxxxxxxx
```

MAY 1

I can't believe it's May already. The cool thing about May is Memorial Day—the first paid holiday of the year. Yay. Instead of thinking of it as a day off with pay, I look at it as an opportunity to make extra $$$ since the paper pays overtime on holidays. Every year I try to sign up to work that day so I can get extra money to...

live. I shouldn't be that dependent on the holiday pay, but I have to earn this money while it's green. Sometimes the editors don't like it when you take on freelance gigs for other sites, saying that it takes away from your real job. But you can always work a holiday shift.

The crazy thing about working on the holidays is that it's either REALLY calm…or REALLY crazy. Memorial Day is definitely a nicer holiday to work than other ones. I really enjoy going to memorials honoring the men and women who have served our country in war…. I always end up covering a salute event and meeting a bunch of veterans from wars as far back as World War II. Miami is crazy busy with tourists during the holiday, anyway, so it's a bit too much to go out, even for a party girl like me. I'd rather try to earn the extra money—it comes out to about an extra $200. I've been doing pretty well with my bills, but the unexpected trademark fee that I paid ($375) to get Frugalista trademarked at the end of March has me feeling a little bit tight in the wallet. I'm still decreasing the debt goblin(s) but it's a day-to-day struggle. This month's overtime $$$ are going to help me pay for my journalism convention registration, which I haven't bought yet. So, things are getting a bit stressed, but after I work this overtime, I will be in financial chillaxing mode.☺ Let's hear it for the vets!

Oh, wait. I forgot. So glad I'm writing this and not saying this: I forgot I have to buy a Mother's Day gift. Eek. I can't stiff Mama McNeal on the gift. It's her favorite holiday. I wonder why? Heh. Yeah, I'll be spending money this month.

MAY 2

Yippee! The government gave me a $600 tax rebate just for living/ breathing…and paying taxes. It hit my account today. Perfect timing. I pray I don't run wild with it. Thank you, Uncle Sam.

MAY 3

To keep the money stream flowing in, not out, I decided to write a freelance article on how Facebook is sucking up my time for TheRoot.com.

I can earn another $200 from my living room if it gets picked up. My college homegirl works there, so I think I have a good chance of getting it published. And yep, that means I will be published again by the Washington Post Company (they own TheRoot.com). Heehee! Best of both worlds: Miami weather and *Washington Post* check. ;)

MAY 4

I love shrimp and cheese grits. It's one of the few things I make really well—props to myself. So, there I was in the Publix cheese aisle, carefully studying my cheese options. I grew up on Kraft, so I was peeping at that brand's array of shredded cheese. Out of nowhere, a woman appeared next to me and said, "Get the store brand! It's on sale." And then POOF, she was gone. Whoa! My own frugal fairy. I walked out with a 4-ounce bag of Monterey Jack and cheddar blend for $2 less than the Kraft brand. There seems to be a brotherhood/sisterhood thing going on among consumers these days. We're all looking out for each other's backs. Oh, frugal fairy, where are you? I want to thank you!

Could the frugal fairy tell that I'm trying to work on my finances? Is Frugalista stamped on my forehead? Maybe it's just a sign of the times. I'm starting to think there's this underground society of Frugalistas. I like it!

MAY 6

The cool thing about my blog is that people email me things all the time. For some reason, everyone looks at me as the freebie lady. My readers (I LOVE the way that sounds. EGO! EGO!) are forever sending in information about coupons, freebies and other deals. I also log on to Slickdeals.net to find out good freebies in town.

I love throwing all the freebies into my blog. I can almost hear the readers rejoicing over the internet. It's crazy what things people value. I am not a coffee drinker, but post something about free Dunkin' Donuts coffee, and the crowd goes wild.

Whenever I am talking to someone new, I always make sure to tell them about my blog and its freebies. I swear, it really makes people like you more, because everyone thinks I've come bearing gifts. Heehee. Yay for frugal networking.

When it comes to the freebie hierarchy, free food gets top ranking. Sure, people like music downloads and beauty products, but EVERYONE agrees on a free meal. I had no idea that so many people eat at McDonald's. If I mention a Mickey D's chicken sandwich giveaway, I'm everyone's new best friend.

I admire everyone's patience when waiting in long lines for the deals. If they have the time to do it, God bless them. I prefer the music and beauty freebies. Whenever there's a free concert, though, I make it a point to find metered parking. In Miami parking garages and private lots can damage your wallet. Also, a lot of these free venue places have CRAZY prices on drinks. What's the point of a free concert if you spend potentially $20 on parking and another $20 on an amaretto sour that would be $8 anywhere else? Frugalista tip: Enjoy freebies, but make sure they remain as close to free as possible. If you have to pay $20 parking fees, is it really free?

The art to freebie pimpin' is finding the stuff that's close to home and easy to get. If you are driving for a freebie and burning up gas, it needs to be something like an Erykah Badu concert, which you would have paid to go to, anyway.

I know the local comedy club that I love down here often gives its frequent users (like me!) free tickets. I love the free tickets but I know it's a 2-drink minimum coming in the door. What they don't advertise is that the 2 drinks could be 2 bottled waters instead of 2 rum and Cokes or shots of Patrón. Tricky, tricky, these places are.

There's an art to this Frugalista thing and it often means asking a lot more questions than you normally would.

MAY 8

Mother's Day. Mama McNeal's getting an airline gift card for $100. She helps out with my niece, Madison, who lives in Nashville. This flying granny nanny doesn't want a robe, a bottle of perfume or dinner in a crowded restaurant. She wants the gift of time. Time with her grandbaby. Sometimes I feel a little guilty that I don't do more for my mother. She's really been supportive of me down through the years—emotionally and financially. She was the biggest fan of my going away to Howard University, a private college in Washington, D.C., despite the fact that I had a really good scholarship to the University of Illinois, which would have guaranteed that I wouldn't be a financial burden on my family. But my mother encouraged me to go where I really wanted to go and assured me that the rest would work out. She tutored kids after school to help with my college bills. Even though I have a student loan from college, it isn't nearly as bad as some of my friends'. I am thankful to my mother for always trying to support my true dreams and teaching me not to settle. I wonder how much her many sacrifices impacted her financially. She has never told me how much she earned as an educator. She's retired now and she doesn't discuss how much she gets from her pension. She never discusses her bills with me. I know after my parents divorced, she had to change her lifestyle. No more weekly hair salon appointments or shopping sprees. She doesn't seem to mind, though, and she doesn't complain. That's a good place to be in, I think. I admire her.

MAY 9

Aw, man, the price of postage stamps is going up again. I'm minivexed about this. Why is this happening? I pay most of my bills, but not all, online. My personal checks cost $20 every time I order them. I'm thinking this last stamp price increase may make me start paying all my bills online.

I was hesitant to sign up for online bill pay through the bank because I felt like it would wed me to the institution. But going to several sites just to pay my bills is worrisome, too. I'm going to stick it to the man! No more mail for me. I'm e-billing. And saving time and money (and trees).

I met Paula, the beauty blogger, for lunch today. Paula picked out a cute Ethiopian café with $7 sandwiches just outside of down-town Miami. I'm so glad we met at the journalism panel a few months ago. It's nice to have someone to talk to about blogging, writing and working for newspapers. Not everyone understands the blogging thing. Paula keeps saying that I need to take my blog independent so I can have total control over it.

She makes some good points. The paper could shut me down at any moment. To its credit, the editors haven't tried to censor me at all. I post what I want and I don't have to get approval. Since my blog is doing well at the paper, I think it's helping me stay employed. Everything is going online and to have a blog at the paper is a good thing. I admire how Paula built her blog totally on her own. I'm going to keep my blog camping at the *Miami Herald* for now. I'm just trying to maintain until I figure out my next career step.

I've been networking a bit more with other online personali-ties, and I have lunch scheduled with Alexis, the author who I met on Facebook who is coming to Miami to finish penning her latest novel. I'm just keeping my options and networks open. Every time I talk to people who I work with, they keep warning about layoffs coming soon. Ugh. How do you remain loyal enough to your job to *keep* your job while figuring out what to do with the rest of your life?

MAY 10

I got THE email. I was not looking forward to it, but in an odd way, I was thinking about it. I knew the call/email/text would come and it did. Cliff's older brother emailed me to say that Cliff died at 3:03 a.m.

I knew when he was checked into hospice care how the story was going to end. I had no idea that you aren't fed when you are in hospice. They just make sure you are comfortable. Something about that disturbed me. I didn't like the waiting. I didn't like that he was dying. I am so hurt that he is gone. He is really gone. He's dead.

Everyone is talking about a memorial for him in Baltimore. Bryant said that I could stay with him at his Baltimore apartment. I know that would cut down on expenses, but I doubt I can make it up there. Flights are under $200, but the cost isn't really the issue (for once). I met Cliff when he was a visiting student at my college. He was such a good writer. He and I kept in touch for years. Even though we have, I mean had (damn, past tense), many of the same friends, by and large, our friendship was just us. I can't see remembering him with people we didn't spend time with together. I think I already said my goodbye when I went to see him in March. I'm sure the memorial service will be moving and well done, but still, it's another goodbye and I cannot handle any more goodbyes this year.

For everything going right in my life—my blog, my health, my friends—this year is shaping up to be one of the strangest. I am the happiest person who is crying. How in the hell did that happen? And why didn't Cliff tell me sooner how bad things really were? I'm not sure why this had to happen. I hope he knew that he was loved. That's all any of his friends could offer in the end. I pray that it was enough.

MAY 12

The *Baltimore Sun* ran an obit about my friend Cliff. It's so wild to read an obit about someone who is (um, was) a peer. I wonder if it was hard for the reporter to write about another journalist, knowing we would all be reading behind him? Cliff covered sports, and we all know that sports writers love to turn a phrase. I know some pretty influential people will read that obit. I wonder if Cliff was able to read it, wherever he is? What did he think? Was he secretly thinking, I could have written it better, like most of us journalists do? Odd to think of anyone having the final word on your life when you've spent your life giving the final word.

Cliff led a disciplined, good life. He should be proud of what he accomplished. Despite what he was going through, he never complained. I remember talking to him about my career woes. He didn't indulge me. He just said, "If you want a new job, send out your résumé and get a new one." Simple, right?

I can't believe I complained to him about my career, given the totality about what he was facing. I mean really. If I knew then....

MAY 13

Fun, fashionable and frugal is my mantra. What else is there to life? I mean, my readers revolt at squandering money but are sure up to see a free concert or two. It's the best of both worlds. I caused a Blouse-gate scandal on my blog because I bought a $16 blouse! I refuse to hold my shame over that one! Frugalista tip: You don't have to give it all up in order to pay off debt and buff up your savings. My philosophy is to enjoy my life as much as possible, while minding the bank. Miser McNeal will never be my name. I don't mind blabbing about balances on my credit cards or how I couldn't go out to play, because I'm trying to save a buck or two. Financial freedom works better for me. Since I've taken a vow of frugality, I feel much more focused.

In the personal finance blogging world, paying off debt is a big old carnival on the internet. I am so glad I started blogging. It's like group therapy, but you can go to sessions anytime, anywhere. A few bloggers have recently paid off their debts. One blogger went from $37,614 down to $8,998 in debt. Certainly, saving money is not a new concept, but somehow it got placed on the back burner for far too many. Frugal capitalism is good. We can all benefit from this "new" trend of earning more and cutting expenses.

I'm glad that speaking/blogging/writing about not becoming prey to subprime loans, credit cards or extravagant lifestyles is en vogue. It's overdue.

MAY 14

TheRoot.com ran my freelance article yesterday. I feel $200 coming my way. Watch out, Visa! I got some money coming to break you down!

MAY 15

I had lunch with Alexis the author today. I drove down and met her in South Beach, where she is staying while she finishes her novel. I met her at the Big Pink diner. It's not superexpensive and the food is decent. I think I've officially become a "lady who lunches." But how else am I going to network with new people? A lot of people who are into handling business don't want to hang out at the local discotheque.

I wore my romper from Shopbop.com that I got on sale last year. I normally can't afford to shop at that site, but the sale was ridiculous and the navy romper was super trendy. And I broke out my Gucci sunglasses.

The sun kissed our shoulders as we met over omelets and orange juice. All the while she was talking, I was thinking, *I. Want. This. Life. This writer's life.* They get to work from home. I don't know anyone who works from home. My friends and I have to report to desk jobs. I am the person with the most freedom, because I get to be in the field, reporting. Now, that doesn't sound so glamorous. I want to be able to write from an exotic location! I live in South Florida, and I get to party at night, but I most certainly don't get to write by the beach. I write by the glaring eyes of Boss Lady, harassing me about a deadline!

I am not a jealous person. Really, I'm not. I have a good life, but again…I. Want. Her. Life. Okay, maybe not *her* life, because I don't know all the details, but I want more options. Sometimes I feel like I'm always twisted in a knot, worried about work, money, whatever.

How can I be the woman by the beach, creating her masterpiece?

MAY 16

I talked to my coworker Paul, who has been working in the burbs more often, and told him that while I want to go to the journalism convention this summer, I'm a little worried about how I will pay for it.

He threw a hissy fit and said that I HAD to go to promote my blog. Promote my blog? How do you promote a blog at the convention? And what could my blog get from the convention? I'm the one who is going, not my blog. Right? He makes it sound like my blog is a business. I'm trying to promote Natalie. Maybe my blog and Natalie are one and the same? Or is my blog becoming a small child that needs care, feeding and conventions?

My blog is about me decreasing debts, not running up debts to promote it, right? Then again, this blog is about the only thing that has me shining right now, and it's the only thing I'm passionate about professionally. In a perfect world, I'd do it full-time.

Paul thinks my blog saved me from getting the ax during the last round of layoffs, because it's new media. Blogs are new media? I've been reading blogs for years, especially the gossip blogs at my desk at work. (Heehee.) Aren't they a way of life for most people?

MAY 22

Three-day weekends can be dangerous for a Frugalista budget. There are so many (expensive) things to do that can empty your wallet in no time. With a 3-day weekend right around the corner, I'm really going to plan my schedule so I don't burn up too much cash.

Here's how I'm watching my dollars:

Thursday evening: Going to see NPR host Diane Rehm speak. The event won't cost me anything, but gas will be a killer. It's about 25 miles away, but it's still worth going. Diane Rehm is smart and foxy. I want to be her when I grow up. Let's hear it for the womanhood!

Friday evening: One of my best friends, Mike, invited me and some other folks out for drinks. The hangout is at a trendy place, which means $14 martinis and $20 shots of Patrón. I'm going to nurse 1 glass of Riesling all night. I think the wine will be under $10. Still, this night has the great potential to be a money trap.

Saturday: Bryant's going to be in town, and he's taking me to a Marlins game and then to a concert to see Lisa Lisa from Cult Jam. He's coming down to Florida quite a bit and it's good for me. It's nice to hang out with the opposite sex. I can eat at home before I go, so Saturday won't be too costly. I'm glad that Bryant is keeping in touch even after the death of our friend. It's nice to have a new friend.☺

Sunday: *My trademark attorney is having a party for his birthday. It's $20 at the door, but since it's for a charity, I can write it off on my taxes. It's at one of those cool lounges/quasi clubs with no roof. Yes, only in Miami do we party with no roofs. Yay for balmy weather. The party is a good 20 miles away from home, but I can't miss it. I think there will be other professionals there. You just never know who you might meet! Gas will be a killer, but parking is plentiful and cheap in that area. The $20 is well worth it.*

Monday: *While everyone is grilling, I'll be working. I can't let the overtime opportunity pass me by. My social life and credit cards could use the discretionary income.*

Even though I'm not going out of town, I still feel like I have travel expenses, because of all the driving I will be doing. This high-priced gas situation is a mess.

MAY 23

Okay, so I lied about working this holiday. I just found out that due to budget constraints, there will be NO OVERTIME. AACKKKK! I'm mini-screwed. I needed that extra money to help pay for the journalism convention registration. I already missed the early bird discount deadline. If I had been diligent, I would have saved $50.

Never in all my years of working has holiday overtime pay been cut. Oh, no. This is an ugly sign of the times. I know the paper industry is having problems, and cutting overtime beats layoffs. But I'm worried that there will soon be layoffs on top of the overtime cuts. It's making me think that this is much more than just a "rough patch."

I know that I have become a bit too overtime dependent, which is the first sign that your finances aren't in order. Still, I wish

I had known sooner that the overtime had been cut. I was really counting on that money.

I know I have a freelance check coming by snail mail any day now, but I'm worried that it's not enough to absorb the upcoming convention costs. Why is traveling so expensive? I know one thing is for sure: I'm not buying any new clothes for the summer convention!

I'm staying home tonight. I need to clean up my darn place and think. When things get stressful, I clean my apartment. It keeps me occupied and stops me from spending money.

Every time I go through my shelves, I feel like an idiot. Why do I have several bottles and containers of the same thing? How in the hell did I end up with 3 bottles of hot sauce for ONE person?

One time while on a cleaning tear, I discovered a calculator underneath my nightstand and an earring I thought I had lost. I swear, I could open a store on eBay with all the "lost" stuff I find during cleaning frenzies.

MAY 24

Despite the financial setback, I am officially at peace with my decision to go to the convention. Mom said she has a free airline pass I can use. It won't be the most affordable thing I've done this year, but I need to attend the convention. They are offering some video editing courses and I'd like to take one. Add another skill to my résumé. Also, since the convention's in Chicago, I'll stay at my mom's house. I have to make it work. And that overtime cut was pretty telling. I need to get out there and hustle more. If I got laid off from my job, that would REALLY kill my budget—much more than a trip to a convention.

Bryant stopped by the house and we went to see the Marlins play but it was a rainy mess. I love live baseball, so I was looking forward to the game. Bryant had to buy me a $5 poncho, which was so kind of him. I met his sister, too, who also went to Howard U. Looking like 2 drowned rats, Bryant and I went to Hooters by my house for dinner. I paid for dinner. He's been really kind through everything and a welcome distraction from this crazy year. The least I could do was buy him a basket of hot wings. LOL

MAY 25

Just got back from the attorney's party. He was so sweet. He waived my cover to get in, so I didn't have to pay the $20. I would have paid, but he was working the door and ushered me and my coworker Teresa through the door.

The crowd was attractive but there were WAY too many women in the house. Teresa bought my drink while we were there, even though I didn't ask her to. Are people thinking I'm on skid row because I write about money issues? Meh. I bought my own drink that night, too. A $12 glass of wine. She bought the first drink, and I got my second. I probably didn't need a second drink, but I was in party mode.

One song came on in which the hook was, "She ain't got no money in the bank." Teresa said it was my theme song.

Ouch! I am not asking for handouts. I pay my own bills. I filed her remark in my mental Rolodex. I hate it when people make digs. Frugalista tip: Be careful who you let buy your drink. People may offer you things for free, but they may be making judgments about you while doing it.

MAY 27

Upon joining Team Frugalista, I made a plan to spend at least $200 per month paying off my credit card bills. I've kept up with that plan and I haven't abused the cards since my frugality vow. I think I may be able to abolish the credit card debt in a year and a half. The car and student loans, well, that's another story. Unless my fortunes change, it's going to take a little longer for them. I already save automatically through my 401(k) at work. But I know I can do better if I practice penury.

For instance, this past weekend I didn't spend a lot of cash, but I did buy a drink at the bar for $12. Maybe I should have had a Coke? Part of being frugal and fabulous is maintaining your budget and your lifestyle. Can I really do both?

MAY 28

Cable TV can be expensive, especially considering how few channels I actually watch. I am guilty. I fought against cable for years, and I finally got it in January so I could watch *The Wire* and CNN. Now that I have it, I really watch only CNN, Bravo and the Style Network. Still, I hold on to cable service. I have a bundled package that includes my internet and phone service for $122. Am I getting ripped off? For all my chatter about saving money, why do I still have cable?

I seemed to live just fine without it for years. I wish there were a way to get just those 3 channels without paying for the whole package.

MAY 29

Throwing a party doesn't mean *paying* for the party, right? It's been a little bit heavy for me this year, so I'm going to throw myself a party in honor of my blog. I threw a party last fall in South Beach and it was SOO much fun. I have spent many a night at clubs east of the Mississippi, so I've seen the best parties. The party I threw in the fall had 2-for-1 drinks, free entry and free appetizers. I threw it with Marika's good friend Robert, who organizes a monthly gathering for professionals. Not to toot my own horn *toot toot*, but my party was SOO hot last year. Everyone gave me props and was begging for my email list of people I invited. Ugh, not a chance. It takes years of click clacking, hanging out, partying, friend making, relationship building to throw a successful party right out of the gate. I share my list with no mortal. Robert is more than happy to negotiate the deal with the venue as long as I bring the bodies. Fair deal!

So anyway, I need to do something to keep myself busy. I need something to pick myself up, and after throwing that party last year, I felt really accomplished. Plus, when you throw a party, it raises your profile. People see you as someone to know. I want to step out of the shadows more. And I'm tired of all the parties in South Beach and their prerequisites for entry. All the party promoters do is invite females to the party with a few men. I HATE that. If men want to look at pretty women, shouldn't women have the option of looking at pretty men—and more than the same 3 of them? It's time for a night-life market correction. Furthermore, I am a grown woman. I don't have to wait for someone else to throw the party I want. I can throw it myself.

I talked to the local journalism group and asked them if it would be okay if I threw a party for my blog with their name attached. The boss said yes. Yay! Robert and I worked out the same deal, but a new location. We are having it at a Chinese restaurant and it's going to have $5 valet parking. So many of these businesses are hurting—even in South Beach—they will practically give you the kitchen sink if you can bring bodies in.

Free appetizers, 2-for-1 drinks and discount parking? Frugal and fabulous! Frugalista power!

CHAPTER 6

June

DEBTS

xxxxxxxxxxxxxxxxxxxxxxxxxxxxxxxxxxxxxx

CREDIT CARDS: $7,962.81

CAR LOAN: $7,192.14

STUDENT LOAN: $2,391.32

xxxxxxxxxxxxxxxxxxxxxxxxxxxxxxxxxxxxxx

TOTAL DEBTS: $ 17,546.27

xxxxxxxxxxxxxxxxxxxxxxxxxxxxxxxxxxxxxx

JUNE 2

In a jewelry box drawer, under my hoop earrings, I found a gift card my coworker Cindy bought me for my birthday. I must have thought the gift card was one of the credit cards I tucked away. Go figure. It's for $25! Yay! I need some new makeup, so this will go to good use. I don't usually wear that much makeup. Healthy skin normally is my mantra. But I feel I should upgrade and polish my appearance a bit more. I'm not a kid anymore, and I so liked the response I got being on CNN. I know I need to invest more in my looks. I want to get dolled up a bit more.

I went to Macy's today and picked out some foundation by MAC. That gobbled up my $25 gift card in seconds. At least I bought something other than a new T-shirt. The good thing is that I can recycle the foundation container, and if I return a set number of old MAC makeup containers, I get a free lipstick.

When I told the sales associate that I couldn't afford the brushes at MAC, she whispered that it's fine to use a cheaper one from the drugstore. Nice, since that cut into her commission. Maybe she's a Frugalista, too?

I'm going to stick with my L'Oréal mascara. It works just fine and costs less than $10. Mascara has to be replaced every 3 months at least. As much as I want to look polished and more camera ready, I know I can't afford $30 or even $20 mascara. Maybelline has a clear version of its Great Lash Mascara, which I can use to groom my wolf-like eyebrows. Now that I'm not running to the salon to get my eyebrows waxed, I need to focus on making them behave. I refuse to pay for overpriced eyebrow gel from the department store. Maybelline is my friend.

So for now, I'm going high-end with the foundation and lip color. But for eyeliner, mascara and brushes, I'm going mass-market. Frugalista tip: Don't always go for the most expensive makeup. With some makeup, like mascara, it is better to buy cheap brands. I haven't bought eye shadow in a really long time. I have a bunch that I need to use before I replenish. I should be okay because it is powder and lasts longer—up to 3 years, I've read. I'm still eye shadow fresh! I have some charcoal shadow that I can use as an eyeliner in a pinch, if I go for a more dramatic look.

JUNE 3

Now that I've got saving money down, I've been thinking about how to make more of it. The blogosphere is abuzz about frugal capitalists—

people who cut back expenses and make it a point to earn more money. While I'm really enjoying not wasting my money, I have to try to earn more cash. Frugalista tip: It's not enough just to stop eating out and getting regular manis. If you really want to make moves, you also have to earn more money.

I've been side hustlin'—doing more freelance articles—for $200 a pop. And if overtime ever shows up again at the paper, I will be first in line. Yes, I have to pay taxes on the money, but I still come out ahead. Because I'm more picky about where I spend my time socially, and I'm not just going out for the sake of going out, I have more time to complete projects that earn income. I'm going only to quality parties and, well, throwing my own. I am investing my time, not just spending it!

I used to freelance for other departments at work, but now I'm writing for other blogs and publications. It gives me the opportunity to get an outside perspective on my work and see how I stack up against others outside of the newsroom. And it gets my name out there.

Yeah, so of course, it's always best to live within your means, but sometimes you want to have more means. I wonder, though, if I made $20,000 more, would I spend a lot more or save a lot more? Would I still have debt, but with a nicer apartment or better car? This digging out of debt business isn't fun, so I don't think I would spend that much more now. If this were pre–no-buy month and pre-blog, I know I would answer that differently—I was planning on an international vacation to celebrate my next salary bump. But now I think the key is to earn more and save more. I have to repeat that to myself. *Earn more. Save more. Earn more. Save more....*

Anyway, things are looking good for The Frugalista Files blog party. My friends are shocked that I'm pulling off a free party with drink specials, appetizers and affordable valet parking in South Beach. I don't have a sponsor. I just have the right connections. So there!

I've pretty much harassed every person on my email list and the journalism association's list into attending, so the numbers should be good. I told the journalists to bring their cameras so I could focus on greeting the guests and being a socialite. I mean, journalists love to report and chronicle, right? They can capture the moments of my jammie! Up with free labor! I'm going to do a slide show with all the photos I gather from the party. A few days ago I went to a party at Marika's condo building and made sure to smile at every guy there and invite him to come out, so ratios should be favorable for the *chicas*. There were some nice men there wearing suits. I hit up a financial planner and a pharmaceutical sales guy. Nice pickings in that neighborhood. I need to live in one of those new condos so I can meet interesting people every day. Then again, maybe I don't want to live in those expensive high-rises. Just to rent one is $1,500, which is $500 more than what I pay a month, which is $6,000 more out of my bank account a year. Whew! (When did I become such a bean counter?)

June 5

When I got my government economic stimulus check, I had a lofty goal of using the $600 to make a dent in the credit card debt. But it was more like $400. I swear, the check got gobbled up somewhere between filling up my gas tank and buying food. Seriously. The good thing about having the money was that it was a stress-free month. The worrisome thing is that the check was a treat. It's not my salary. I need to step up my Frugalista capitalista behavior game big-time. More cutting back, more money coming in.

Gearing up for the big party tomorrow night. I sent out a final email blast to everyone on my list, hyping the party. I told Teresa to bring her camera to take photos. Have my outfit ready to go—thank you, closet shopping—and I have my new MAC foundation ready! Operation Hostess with the Mostest. (I'm so corny!)

June 7

OMG! My party last night was so awesome! I wore a purple sleeveless shirt with a black exposed zipper in the back and black slacks.

My look was flirty but still comfortable. I had to be the hostess with the mostest! I warmed my hair over with a flatiron, so it was cute. I didn't get it done professionally, even though I think it would have been a worthwhile splurge. I just didn't have time to plan the party and sit in a chair at a salon. Time is money!

God bless that DJ. He played the best hip-hop and funk music ever. Judging by the dancing and two-stepping that occurred later on, people seemed to vibe to his music. Well, maybe it was the DJ or the 2-for-1 drinks that had everyone joyful?! Whatever the case, it worked. We took over the restaurant. The night was so busy, I didn't even get a chance to eat. I got there early to greet the guests, so I didn't even have to pay $5 for valet parking. I just used the parking meter. Frugalista power.

The party had two shifts of people: the after-work crowd and the true partyers. For the first 2 hours, I got a lot of working professionals looking to network with the journalists. I even had a few college students who were looking for job opportunities. Welcome to the club! I had to make sure to introduce the college kids to some of the more seasoned journalists who could help them with their careers. I wanted to make sure they stayed at the party as long as possible. I hate to sound like a "social madam," but everyone loves young, smart and cute eye candy at a party. If they stayed longer, then the other guests would want to stay, too. I had made sure to invite every cute guy I knew (or met leading up to the big night), so I knew we would be sufficient with the number of eligible men, but I wanted to make sure we had enough girls to keep the guys entertained. Geppetto has nothing on my (party) puppet master skills!

Vivian and Marika brought a lot of friends. Good work, ladies. I think Marika invited every attorney in South Florida. I have a pretty good party list, but it's always good to have friends who can pack the crowd with their own (interesting) friends. A few of the cuties from the earlier party came through. One of them was a true party guy. He went into a dance battle with a coworker, and the two of them went into a dirty dancing routine (okay, maybe not that wild with the running lift, but the guy threw my friend's leg over his shoulder and spun her around). I'm not mad about it. Whatever it takes to keep the guests entertained! He'll be invited to my next party. Heh. My friend Marc invited people from his urban professional Meetup.com group, so we had a nice, full crowd.

Drinking-wise, I was well cared for. Heehee. One of the cute guys, Dan, the pharmaceutical sales manager from Marika's party, bought me a drink, which was awesome. Okay, maybe I have a crush on Dan, so whatever he does is awesome. I couldn't tell if he was buying me the drink because he was being nice or because he might be interested. Either way, I'm so happy that he came to my party. He said that he would. Good sign, right? Marika's his neighbor, so I'm going to ask her for more details on him later.

One of my guy friends, Christopher, who works for the state attorney's office, tried to hook me up with a guy, Ralph, who works in investing or at a bank or something. I wasn't sure. I exchanged numbers with the guy, who was fine as hell. (Broad shoulders. Flat stomach. Clearly, he works out. 'Nuff said.) We'll see. Hopefully, he will call, but I didn't like that Christopher had to be the matchmaker. If Ralph were really interested, wouldn't he have tried to talk to me on his own? Christopher swears that Ralph asked him about me at the party. Still, I have little patience for the homeboy hookup. Dude is going to have to call me first. He is nice looking, though. We didn't get to chat much at the party, even though I tried to engage. Maybe he was shy?

My colleague Teresa talked to Ralph's friend Frank for quite a while at the party, too. I've seen Frank at a few other social settings and Frank is married. The asshole didn't wear his wedding ring to my party and I'm sure he didn't mention his wife. How pathetic. Miami is too small for secrets. I'm going to have to tell Teresa to proceed with caution. She's still pretty new in town and is still meeting people. If Frank was getting a divorce, I would have heard about it. I think Teresa got her first clue at the end of the night, when we talked outside of the club and some of Frank's coworkers just happened to be walking by from another club and asked him loudly how his son was doing in front of Teresa. SCANDAL.

I can't wait to upload the photos and get everyone else's photos from the night. I want to do a photo slide show for my blog. I'm so blog obsessed. I also want to show off the photos to my friends in Chicago to do a "man review" of the cuties at my party. I tried to be sure to take a shot with all the men candy at the party. I may have missed a few.

Paul from work teased me, saying that I just couldn't throw a party for the journalism organization, that I just had to include my blog. Uh, yeah.

My blog had its first party. It's like a baby having his or her first birthday party! I am one proud mama!

JUNE 12

My party high didn't last that long. I guess that would be too much to ask of my life: good times all the time. I am on an emotional roller coaster today. We all knew that layoffs were coming soon, but now my friends at work are saying they are coming "any day now." I wonder if Human Resources is leaking the layoff news to the newsroom to prepare us?

I am trying to do my work and focus, but I am friggin' scared. My finances cannot absorb a layoff. How would I earn an income? Outside of my 401(k) I don't really have a savings account. I am a single woman with a single income. I need to find someone to marry right quick! Maybe I will call that guy I met at my party.☺

Everyone at work is freaking out…. In the main newsroom, there's a sacrificial Santeria rooster being offered up on a file cabinet and everyone is leaving baby dolls, candles, money, coins and shiny beads. If the newsroom people are resorting to shrines and offerings to keep their jobs, things are really bad. Do I laugh, or do I cry? I am working at a place where the employees erect sacrificial shrines. I mean, if that isn't a sign that things aren't going well.

I am both fascinated and scared. I called Teresa and told her to walk over to the shrine to check it out. She refused. We are all a bit freaked out. Someone leaked the Santeria shrine out to some news blogs. Some friends called me to get the skinny. I didn't pick up my phone. I couldn't talk about what was going on at work. It was so surreal.

If that wasn't enough, another coworker in my office lit a candle and started walking laps around our office, praying to a higher power and chanting. No one stopped him. I think we were hoping his blessing would extend to all of us, and I'm not even Catholic. We want to keep our jobs, by any means. I know I've complained about my status at work. I've even complained about my check. But I didn't want to be put in a position where the check stopped altogether! This "waiting for a layoff" is killing me inside.

Ugh! I've been to church only a handful of times this year, and I don't tithe. I mean, I've been trying to save money. I don't even belong to a church. I kind of go to the churches I like and enjoy the service. Even if I wanted to start my own praying ritual, which seems to be the craze in the office all of a sudden, I'm not sure if Jesus would want to hear me. I knew I should have slipped more than a $20 bill in the offering plate at church! Does Jesus forgive cheapskates? Gah!

Boss Lady has been spending more and more time in the main office and less time in the bureau. The main office is where the real decisions get made. I've been trying not to piss her off these last few months. There's nothing I can do to change who gets laid off, if the rumors are true that layoffs are coming. Is she in a back office, making deals, telling her editor peers that Natalie needs to get the ax? When will they let us know who is going and staying? After whispers in the office about the pending layoffs, I want to know if I have a job or not. I can't take this. This year has been so up and down. A relationship that ended, after a Disney World trip, no less. My friend dies. I create an awesome blog. A CNN appearance. And now sacrificial offerings at the job.

All I wanted to do was write a few articles that would change the world, earn me a Pulitzer and allow for middle-class bliss in a cool city. Now I need a prayer ritual to get through the day! My stomach was in a knot for the whole rest of the day.

Some people in the office played the "guess who will get let go" game, taking guesses on who they think will get the ax. Some reporters are typing in bylines in the computer, finding out who filed the most stories.

I feel vulnerable. A few of the reporters say they think I am safe because of my blog. They say I have been creative and have shown that I have "multimedia" skills. I think my blog helps. But I'm still not sure that I am sacred, er, safe.

It sucks not knowing if I'm the sacrificial employee. Please, Ma Herald. Make the announcement, all ready. I hate being in limbo.

JUNE 16

Ugh. D-day at work again. Another round of staff reductions. Aw, man. These are more aggressive than the last round. One person has to leave from my reporter class, which is how we are divided up. I'm like at level two out of four levels and someone out of the level twos has got to go. My desk mate Julia is on the list. Ugh. She has worked on and off for the paper for years, even longer than I have worked here, but when they calculate seniority, you're ranked by your last start date. After taking time off to travel and start her family, Julia ranks low in terms of seniority. Although I have complained about working here for so long, I am in a good position seniority-wise. Crazy how that goes.

We'll know by next week how it all shakes out.

We've had buyouts before. It's the economy and our industry. I know I'm in a good position to not get laid off, for now. If the paper is going by seniority for the layoff target list, I'm in a stronger position because I've been at the paper almost 8 years. It's funny that just a few months ago, I looked at staying at my job a long time as a horrible thing. And now it has worked in my favor!

But what's up with my future? Plan A is to work as long as possible at the *Miami Herald*. I've been here awhile and I know the landscape. It's a good paper. I have my blog here, which, quite honestly, keeps me going. The last thing I need right now is to lose my main source of income. My strategy to keep my job: get along with everyone at the office, do as I'm told with a smile and push this blog thing as far as it can go. I wonder if I get extra work points for throwing a hot party for my blog? Also, the editors seem to like the videos that I've been posting on my blog. *More of that, Nat. More of that.*

Also, I need to start going down to the main office more. It's where the decisions get made. I know I've been here for ages, but that doesn't mean I can't try to strengthen relationships with the main editors. It can't hurt, right?

So that's Plan A, but career-wise, I still need a Plan B. A real, tangible Plan B. Not this "I'll look for another job" Plan B. I need to figure out how I will live, eat and pay bills if I ever get laid off. The staff reductions are coming more and more frequently. I realize that I may not leave here by choice some day.

A few friends who have seen the news about the layoffs emailed and texted me to make sure I was OK. I told them that I seem to be in a good position for now. Oh, yes, they wanted to talk about the sacrificial rooster at the main newsroom. Only in Miami!

JUNE 17

Drinks and early dinner in downtown Miami, at Blue Martini, with Teresa. Teresa works in the main office and I was going to meet her there but opted to wait outside. Everyone is so pissed off about the layoffs, it's best that I not go inside the building. I know I said I wanted to work on getting to know the main editors better, but I need to wait until the dust settles from the layoffs. Everyone is a bit, ahem, preoccupied.

Teresa and I found a half-off special on drinks and food, so we're taking advantage of it. She hasn't worked long at the paper and her department has been targeted for layoffs, but she doesn't know if she's going to be axed. She's in management and says it's hard having middle management jobs. They are the first to get the squeeze at work because they pay so much. I know her salary is more than double my salary. It's a shame that I feel comforted at earning less money—that makes me less of a target at work.

I still want to earn more, though. It's better to get laid off from a six-figure job than one that pays $44,000, right? I'd hope that I'd have a decent savings account if I was making twice as much. Does it have to be that the more money you make, the more money you spend? But then again, people would think with my stable work history and being single with no kids that I'd have my finances in better order.... On the other hand, I don't have a shared income to help with overhead.

The bottom line is that nowadays most of us need to work—married or not—and a lot of us aren't where we want to be financially. A lot of the editors at work are underwater on their home mortgages. And these people aren't lavish. I swear Hondas are the official car of the newsroom. But the housing crisis is no joke.

My mother always says you can't count other people's money. It's true. You just don't know what other people have going on in their bank accounts. Until recently, I didn't know what was up with my bank account, either. Frugalista tip: Everyone can have financial problems. It doesn't matter how much you earn.

I paid for dinner. I don't want Teresa to leave. She just got to Miami. Teresa was pretty bummed. We all are bummed. The whole industry is bummed. That sacrificial rooster can't save us.

JUNE 19

Death to the latte! And it's about time. Middle-class Americans are dropping their $4 lattes and brewing coffee at home. This is a step in the right direction. A story I read on the Associated Press did the math on the cost of buying a bottle of soda every weekday for a year: "A $1.50 bottle of soda for each weekday of the year, for example, would add up to about $390. Now at $2 in some parts of the country, the habit comes with an annual price tag of $520. Over 5 years, that's $2,600."

Yikes! It all adds up. I know that Starbucks has taken a financial hit in this economy and plans to close some stores this year. I doubt I'd notice. Is it just me or are those green logos on every corner? The company has beefed up its rewards program to try to keep its fans. It offers free Wi-Fi for its habitual users. You still have to watch your budget. Frugalista tip: If you are serious about saving, don't drink away your budget on coffee or soda. Water is free—drink it instead, and you can save thousands a year.

JUNE 24

I have to step it up financially. I have to get on top of filing for reimbursement on work-related expenses. As a journalist, I drive around, chasing stories, burning gas and "wearing and tearing" my car. I pay for photocopies of public records. I pay for parking while on stories. I use my cell phone to check in with editors. Now ask me, am I diligent? Do I file for reimbursements from the company? No. Meh! When life gets so hectic, you tend to forget to sweat the small stuff, like the 15-mile drive you did for work. But it all adds up. I noticed a big difference in my bank account when I filed my expenses weekly. My goal for next month is to do it regularly.

CHAPTER 7

July

DEBTS

xxxxxxxxxxxxxxxxxxxxxxxxxxxxxxxxxxx

CREDIT CARDS:	$7,765.42
CAR LOAN:	$6,907.05
STUDENT LOAN:	$2,342.34

xxxxxxxxxxxxxxxxxxxxxxxxxxxxxxxxxxx

TOTAL DEBTS: $ 17,014.81

xxxxxxxxxxxxxxxxxxxxxxxxxxxxxxxxxxx

JULY 1

In a few days the layoffs will be finalized and Julia will have to leave the paper. An online petition was circulated around work to try to save her job, but it didn't help.

Julia seems to be in good spirits. She talked to Boss Lady, who told her not to look back at the *Miami Herald*. The *Herald* often rehired former employees. I was an intern here before I finished my college degree, worked in a smaller market and then was hired full-time. For Julia to be told not to look back is major. I guess I'm not as safe as I thought I was! I took comfort in knowing that I had longevity at the paper. But I've been at the paper almost 8 years. Many of my coworkers have been here decades. Talk about a wake-up call.

Teresa's job is safe for now, so that's good, but a talented photographer in my office has to go, which makes me miserable. Alfred always used to do sneak little photos of me when we'd be on a story together. If a picture is worth a thousand words, Alfred knows how to take that photo.

In a moment of panic (there have been a lot of those lately), I asked my mother if I could move home if I got laid off. Of course, she's fine with it; what mother doesn't want her baby girl home for a while? I still don't think that's the best Plan B, though…moving home with my mother. My mother and I are close and I know she supports me. However, I know she likes supporting me as an able-bodied working adult. I'm not 100 percent convinced she wants me home without a job or a clear plan. I need a plan. A clear one.

For a person who prides herself on being strategic and having an idea about what she wants to do with her career, I'm kind of floundering. I'm clueless. There, I said it. I don't know how to make a career for myself when there are no jobs. My industry has been suffering for a while, but there's a big difference between slow hiring and NO hiring. Newspapers are becoming extinct.

Many journalists who tire of the newsroom consider public relations jobs. They pay better and journalists certainly have good connections to work. But I can't really see myself working in PR.

After years of working in local news, I really want a job that I truly want to do. I want to be passionate about what I do. I am still passionate about journalism, but not the kind that I practice. I just don't want to end up in another job where I am stuck. I want a career.

The good thing about the day job is that everyone is pitching in to help each other. We're all trying to help our laid-off colleagues find new jobs by sending out job listings. I've also seen a few underground lists of journalism jobs that only a few select people are invited to view. Nice. My eyes and ears are open.

I could always take my blog independent, like my blogger homeys are begging me to do, although I like having it at the *Herald*. I worked hard to build it up. I'm not sure I want to move locations. I bought up a whole bunch of URLs, which I'm just letting sit, unused, until the time is right. To have true blog credibility, you have to launch the blog on your own. But short of getting some serious ad revenue lined up, that doesn't solve the whole income problem. What am I going to do?

JULY 4

I went to my coworker Miguel's for his Fourth of July party with a bunch of other friends and people from the paper. His high-rise condo offered an awesome view of the fireworks. I didn't read the invitation carefully. I brought a bottle of my favorite inexpensive ($6.99) *moscato*. Miguel specifically asked that guests bring something other than wine because he collects wine. Let's just say he has hundreds of bottles and most cost well over $7. I'm so used to bringing my affordable wine from the grocery store everywhere. Oops. Frugalista failure.

Last year on the Fourth, I was at the Essence Music Festival, hanging out with Vivian, my cousins and the rest of the party crew. I had sooooooo much fun last year. We saw Beyoncé and Mary J. Blige perform. We walked everywhere and kept our cups full of whatever spirits we wanted.

It was so different this year, watching fireworks on a friend's balcony. Going to the Essence Music Festival cost me about $700. I had to buy concert tickets, eat and pay for travel.

Yes, I love those memories. Whenever I get nostalgic for the good old bad days, I look at my Visa card balance to remind myself why I brought a $7 *moscato* wine from the grocery store to Miguel's bachelor pad party. It's working for me. Fewer legacy costs. LOL

Someday I'll get back to the occasional party trip, but not anytime soon. Between the layoffs at work, my vow of frugality and my still paltry savings, I'm taking a much-needed time-out.

The evening was lovely. It was nice to kick back, talk and drink with friends I hadn't seen in a while. You can act as silly as you want to without being self-conscious at house parties. Everyone knows you, anyway, unlike at the club. Plus, I love Miami skylines and balcony pimpin'. That's the good thing about having friends who live in nicer buildings than I do: I can reap the benefits of their fab lifestyle when visiting and then go home to my el cheapo place with a view of the parking lot.☺

Having good friends to celebrate the holidays with makes a huge difference in my life. I have only 1 cousin in Miami, so my friends are really my family. So glad I had the option of a house party this year. Clubbin' over holiday weekends is a grind with the random celebrity-hosted parties and the out-of-town people flashing their cash. I live here! I'm not a tourist! I can't keep up with people who have vacation money to burn. I live this life every day. Moderation is key.

JULY 6

First day back after the layoffs. There are still some rumblings about who had to leave and who got to stay. Julia's desk is empty. Everyone used to say that the older people are first to get the cut because they earn more than the younger workers. I'm not sure if Julia's hit 30 yet, and I doubt she made a lot. Reality check: no one is indispensable. The place is clearing out. Amen for having a job, but I'm not so sure about my future in the newspaper business. Trying not to stress about it, but I am dead serious: I need a Plan B. And this Plan B needs to include more than "find another job." From the looks of it, I'm not sure how much longer newspapers and magazines will be around. My paper, quite honestly, waited longer than other papers to cut staff. It's happening everywhere.

JULY 10

Yesterday I wrote a blog post about student loans. Man, from the feedback I received, there are a lot of people dealing with those blessed, yet cursed loans. Loans are a blessing because they allow you to get a college education even if you don't have the cash for it. While they're not considered "bad debt," like credit cards, they are still loans that have to be paid back. I read that many college students are graduating with $20,000 or more in loans!

If you work in a profession where there is a huge need for your services—teaching or nursing— some of your loans may be forgiven, meaning you won't have to pay them back. It all depends on what kind of arrangement your job has. Also, people who volunteer for places like AmeriCorps and the Peace Corps can get their loan balances trimmed down. Unfortunately, there's no student loan forgiveness for journalists.

I graduated from college years ago, so why am I still paying off a $2,300 bill? And it's going to take a while longer. My student loan is like an old boyfriend who just won't go away. We had a good run, but it's time for the relationship to end.

Some of my friends have gone on to graduate school, but I opted not to because I'm still paying for my undergraduate education. Until I pay off the loan and get my budget right, I don't want to take on more debt. I thought about getting an MBA until I read an article that said the degree doesn't guarantee earning more money. Um, that doesn't work for me. In media, education is nice to have on your résumé, but it's not necessary. Some of the best journalists never even went to college but learned on the job.

I will put my student loan to rest soon enough. It's hilarious that my student loan debt is less than my credit card debt now. I've charged up more than I've borrowed for higher education. Talk about mixed-up priorities. Ha!

JULY 12

When I buy clothes, I always buy on sale or off price. Marshalls and T.J. Maxx are near and dear to me. Since taking my vow of frugality, I've bought only about 4 clothing items for a whopping total of $56.64! I've become a big fan of shopping in my closet and swapping clothes with friends. It's amazing how you can pull new looks together! I found this site, Savvycircle.com, and if you write in what you're looking for, the site will alert you when those things go on sale. Thinking I might use the site if I need a cocktail dress in the future. Other than that, I am so out of the retail therapy business.

JULY 13

OMG! I woke up this morning with the absolute worst stomachache. I could barely stand. I could barely sit on the toilet. Any movement caused me to double over in serious pain. And on a friggin' Sunday, too. I was supposed to go to work and meet Lillian to shoot some video for my blog. Ouch! I called my doctor, who told me to run my ass to the emergency room. Okay, he didn't say it like that but that's how I heard it. Clearly, he had concerns. I'm almost never sick. Okay, a bit of a sniffle occasionally. But random this-hurts-like-crazy pain? Ugh.

I called my mother and told her that I was going to the hospital. She told me to call her when I got there. I could barely walk to my car to drive to the emergency room. Of course, when I got there and checked in, I was told I needed to wait. I called Lillian to let her know what was up.

"What? You're at the hospital? Dude, that will make great footage," she said.

Was she crazy?? I'm in pain and I'm at the emergency room! Can't a sister get some sympathy? I don't need to film a reality show! I need medical care and attention. I am alone. These journalists—anything for a story. Ack! And ouch! My tummy!

"Lillian, I'll call you back and let you know," I told her.

I called my mother to let her know I was still waiting at the hospital and that Lillian wanted to come and shoot video.

"Yes, you should let her!" Mom said. What the hell? Is this what young Michael Jackson felt like? I'm surrounded by Joe Jacksons!

After waiting and waiting in the waiting room (oh, I get the name) for ages, I was put into a room to wait (some more) for the doctor. The nurse checked my vitals and had me urinate in a cup to test for pregnancy (ha!). I told her about my tummy. And then the doctor came in. Good Lord. He was GORGEOUS! Cinnamon skin. His hair was a carpet of curls.

"Have you been stressed?" Dr. Sexy asked.

"Yes," I whimpered. "We had layoffs at work. But I wasn't laid off."

"I'm sure you've had to do more work, because productivity normally goes up when people are laid off," Dr. Sexy said.

Oh my God! He's kind and understanding, too. What will we name our children?

"Let's do an exam," Dr. Sexy said.

Yes, let's. Oh, wait. Ugh. An exam down there? Like this? Now? We just met. It's been a while, you know, Dr. Sexy. Only I would get the fine doctor when I needed a pelvic exam and swabbing downstairs. This is so clinical. He's messing with the romance going on in my head. Also, it's clearly time for me to start dating again. Jeez, I'm so random.

After Dr. Sexy performed his doctorly duties, I called Lillian and told her that I was okay with her coming to do the video.

"Dude, what's wrong with you?" was Lillian's introduction.

"Um, I'm sick, I don't know and all you want to do is shoot video," I snapped.

This is surreal. *Suck it up, Nat. It's for your blog.* And that's the only thing that's apparently working right these days.

To shoot the video, I got out of that god-awful white gown that ties in the back, threw back on the swing dress I wore to the hospital and tried to look like I wasn't in obscene pain while lying on a reclining chair.

Naturally, I mentioned I was worried about the emergency room bill. Emergency rooms are expensive! I'll be furious if this random thing throws me off my Frugalista plan. I've got credit card debt to be slayed. And a journalism convention to attend later this month.

"Let's see how today will turn out," I said.

I hope the video was good enough. I'm thankful to have ambitious people supporting me. Even if it means I get filmed while in the emergency room. Too bad I'm not getting paid extra! Lillian, you had better make me look like Lifestyles of the Sick and Glamorous. My blog is about frugal and fabulous living. Not emergency room chic!

"Feel better, man," Lillian said before leaving.

Gee. Thanks, Lillian. Enjoy your Sunday with your friends and family. I'll just nestle here in this sterile room. My doctor will keep me company. He cares for me!

I felt like I'd already been there for 5 days when Dr. Sexy finally came back.

"Well, I think you have a ruptured cyst on your ovary," Dr. Sexy said. "It can be caused by stress. And I'm warning you that you may experience this again if you continue being so stressed."

Are you serious, Dr. Gorgeous? A ruptured cyst? On my ovary? Not one of the ovaries that's waiting for the right guy to come along and make proper use of it?

Dr. Sexy prescribed some pills for pain, told me to visit an ob-gyn within a week and went on his merry way.

Dr. Sexy made his point. I have got to stop being stressed out. Period. I don't want another repeat of this episode. I'll do a follow-up visit with my ob-gyn. Too bad he's not as cute as Dr. Sexy, though.

I can't believe I've been so stressed that I made myself ill. This just doesn't sound good. I am too young to be this stressed about anything going on in my life. I am not a Wall Street banker. They are the people who have stress-related injuries, right? And that kind of stress is a trade-off for making the big bucks. Is this how it all begins? First, a cyst ruptures. Then the eyesight goes. Then the heart attack, followed by a stroke. Then they quit the corporate life and become goatherds on the mountainside in Wyoming…. Here I am in the ER because of stress, and I have yet to crack $50,000 a year!

My poor ovary. I need you. Hang in there—the best is yet to come. And how in the hell am I so stressed out over a job layoff—AND I DIDN'T EVEN GET LAID OFF?? Shouldn't I be happy and relieved and not overly (um, ovary) stressed?

I checked myself out of the hospital. The copay? $300. And it went right onto my debit card. Jeez, I'm going to the poorhouse. Again.

Okay, this makes zero sense: I'm working at my job so I can have health care, and I'm so stressed because of that job that I wind up shelling out $300 for an ER visit, despite the health care? Some shit has got to change. And it will. When I got home, I popped some of the 800 mg ibuprofens that Dr. Sexy gave me.

While the ruptured cyst is something that will heal itself, it has me thinking about my life and what kind of lifestyle I want. It's one thing to get pimples when you are stressed, but it's another to have something that lands you in the hospital for the day. I need a lifestyle change. Clearly. No more ER runs for me.

JULY 14

Everyone at work was nosy, asking about the Band-Aid on my arm from yesterday's little emergency room adventure. Yeah, I went to the hospital because I had a killer stomachache because I'm over-stressed about work. What a mess.

My journalism convention is coming up in another week. I'm going to do some informal laps around the job fair and that's that. I'm starting to think that an exit plan from the newsroom may be in order. My friend Ross says that "journalism is dead." I won't give up all hope, but I'm not sure that looking for another job in another newsroom is the answer. Everyone is laying off: TV, newspapers, broadcast, magazines. I would hate to get a new job in a new city, only to be laid off.

Add to this frustration the fact that I just heard about new fees to check baggage, so now I have to pay even more for a convention that I'm not sure is worth it! And to say that I'm a little vexed about all these new fees would be an understatement. People will find a way to make money on anything! Since I'll be in Chicago for a few days, I'll need to pack plenty of clothes, which means I have to check my luggage. Will I ever learn to travel with one carry-on suitcase? How do people do it? I need all my clothes just in case I have to meet with a recruiter (or Mr. Right) and need to look perfect.

To make sure I don't go over the baggage weight allowance, I'm bringing only my platform sandals for evenings and my black ankle-strap, peep-toe pumps for daytime. Jeez. You'd think the airlines could give a girl a break—it's hard enough to look fashionable on a budget without having to worry about how heavy the baggage is. This Frugalista is determined to look her best without paying extra!

JULY 21

I'm heading to the Windy City for my journalism convention in a few days. So excited! I'm feeling good. No pain from my ovary mishap. Those horse pills worked. I'm back in the saddle. Upward and onward.

I signed up for video training. Webisodes, here we come. A girl has to look good, so I got my hair professionally washed and set for the first time in ages! It was time for my seven-week relaxer, so that expense was in my budget. I can now roller set my hair well. I can give myself a mean hair conditioning treatment by applying olive oil to nourish my dry scalp. But I absolutely refuse to apply lye (the main chemical to relax hair) myself—lye is a serious chemical and I don't trust myself to do it safely or right.

While I'm all for living on less, a girl still has to pamper herself now and then. And sometimes it's important to make an investment in how you look. It's all about balance: while I spent money on my hair, I did give myself an at-home mani-pedi and saved $40. My stylist didn't say much about my sporadic visits, or say that it looked like I was damaging my hair with my new DIY attitude. She was just happy to see me. So far, so good in the Frugalista hair department.

As for what to wear...that's harder. My friend John—we went to Cliff's together—got me into the VIP party, and I'm going to have to look the part. I was planning to wear a shirt (okay, my purple party blouse from my Frugalista jam last month) in my closet to a Thursday night party, but John made it clear that I've been seen in that shirt a few too many times. He also vetoed my go-to black dress. John has turned into a bit of a party tyrant. I've known him for years and I know how he can be, so I just roll with it. He's got a good heart and great fashion sense (rare for a guy, I know). He just gets into party promoter mode and it's over the top.

I've decided that Facebook is bad for Frugalistas. It's hard to throw on your favorite standbys when you have a hundred photos in that same top plastered all over FB! You go out looking your best, take photos, post them online and then everyone sees your hottest gear. Meh.

So I found a cute dress for $30 at Ross. I normally don't shop at Ross but Vivian swears by it for dresses. I figured that I would try something new and there's a Ross down the street from my house. Good Lord, the lines are so long there. That's one thing I don't miss about my shopping habit. LINES! Anyway, I thumbed through the racks and saw a few cute dresses, but this magenta dress called my name. It said, "Natalie, take me with you." Really, it did. I like the way the color looks against my skin. And it's washable. And most importantly, it's affordable! I waited in the long-ass line to buy the dress and didn't retreat. I'll just consider it an investment.

I may try to find another one, too. I do want to look cute while I'm there. I'll be seeing friends I haven't seen in a year and I want to represent. I swear, John's party had better be great or...it just better be great.

To save money, I'll be staying with my mom. She lives in the suburbs, a 25-minute train ride from the convention. While staying at the host hotel is great for meeting and mingling, now's not the time for that. Plus, I don't get to see my mother much. She'll like having me home and I'll be just busy enough so we don't get on each other's nerves. Two grown women in one home is asking a lot—family or not. Meow! Ffft!

Staying at Mom's will save me about $300. I packed one suitcase and found out that my airline allows one piece of luggage to be checked in for free. Frugalista for life!

JULY 27

The convention. I did a few laps in the job fair. I ran into Tanya at the CNN booth. I thanked her again for helping me get on air. While talking to her, she asked me to help her throw a fund-raiser in Miami for our journalism group. That was pretty cool. I love a good party and I need to return the favor for her hooking me up. I guess the word has gotten around about my fiesta skills. I'm pretty darn good at it, if I say so.☺

Had a meeting with a recruiter. It was…interesting. I met the guy at the convention center for a cup of coffee. He bought it and we didn't sit down. The recruiter walked me into the hallway and we stood up and talked. Somehow I don't think if he were really interested in me, he'd make me stand and sip coffee in a hallway. He said he'd introduce me to some of the online people at the company at a reception later on. I'm not quite optimistic.

I networked with some bloggers at a panel on blogging (loved it). I took a video training course. One of the highlights was meeting the executive editor of *Real Simple* magazine. I love that magazine. Turns out, she has her own blog on the side…and she loves The Frugalista Files! Yay! Couldn't believe it! A New York magazine editor reads my blog and likes it enough to link it to her personal blog!

In the hallway at the convention, a few young Turks asked me questions about journalism. They were so cute and bushy-tailed. I remember when…and they were asking me about the industry. Keep blogging, kiddies. Chase those fires. File those cop briefs. Go to city commission meetings, but keep your online presence up. It made me feel good to know what I was talking about.

As for John's party, I didn't stay long. I got caught up party hopping with Teresa and her friends, so I got to John's event super late. I didn't even get in as a VIP. Meh! So much for the party. At least my new dress was seen elsewhere.

I tried not to worry too much about the economy or the industry, but there was a feeling of gloom and doom about the newspaper business at the convention in general. I do want to have a conversation or two with the bosses when I get back to work. What I liked best about being at the convention was learning about how to edit video and hanging out at the blogging panel. I still would like a business journalism job, but I think I may like working only on the web more.

JULY 28

Now that the convention has come and gone, I'm making myself do the Frugalista math.

Here's what the convention would have cost pre-Frugalista:

Registration: $375

Airfare: $300

Parking: $64

Hotel with Roommate: $300

Meals at Chicago Restaurants: $125

Total: $1,164

Here's my new, improved Frugalista costs:

Registration: $275 (I received a $100 stipend from the Miami Herald.*)*

Airfare: $0 (Mama McNeal bought me a plane ticket using her frequent-flyer miles.)

Parking: $55 (I spent no money on daytime parking; see Train Fare below. Nighttime parking in downtown Chicago is out of hand. 'Nuff said.)

Train Fare: $36.55

Hotel: $0 (I stayed at McNeal's Bed-and-Breakfast, in my childhood bedroom.)

Meals: $40 (I ate out only a few times and crashed many a receptions for free nibbles and drinks.)

Clothing: $66 (I ended up buying 2 dresses, which I will wear again and again and again, Facebook photos allowing.)

Total: $472.55

Savings: $691.45!

Do the math! I am a Frugalista for life!

JULY 29

While at my journalism conference, I did some blog networking. I met the blogger from *The Crushed Grape Report*. I learned that she was a Frugalista, and that she wrote an awesome post on affordable wines to drink, which I read later. Yay! See, that's why I had such a great few days at my journalism conference. Where else can you learn about perfecting your craft and finding affordable spirits?☺ I'm going to take some of her advice for the next party I go to so I can make sure to bring wine that's right for my host as well as my budget.

JULY 30

Feeling pretty good about this whole Frugalista thing—just looking over how much I saved at the convention makes me inspired to keep the savings coming. Was thinking about this when I came across a CBS article on how American families waste about $1,200 worth of food a year. Whoa!

Sadly, I totally relate. I find myself tossing my salad in a garbage bag sooner than I'd like. I forget about that yogurt in the back of the fridge that I bought in bulk and on sale, trying to save a dime. Um, I'm not saving any money if I'm throwing out food! I have no plans to become a freegan, but I'm going to take some of these tips from the article to heart:

- Stop buying food in bulk *(with just li'l ol' me, it goes bad too quickly).*

- Shop on Thursday, because you will be around on the weekend to cook. *(I totally agree. I may not be an excellent cook, but I'm a pretty good weekend cook. I'm relaxed and creative on the weekends. On Monday nights, not so much.)*

- Arrange your refrigerator so that the oldest goods are in the front.

I swear, I think I'm a new woman. I never thought I would be this good at the domestic stuff, but there's a part of me wondering why not? I generally like the fact that I can cook. It makes me feel more normal and in sync with everyone. It's not really cute to run around saying you are a grown woman and can't cook. Food, clothing, shelter. I mean, food is a basic necessity. I need to give myself more credit and to try new things. You can be fabulous and throw down in the kitchen. You can wear heels and know how to style your hair. You can have and do it all, if you have to. And, let's face it. I do!

CHAPTER 8

August

```
DEBTS

xxxxxxxxxxxxxxxxxxxxxxxxxxxxxxxxxxxx

CREDIT CARDS:   $7,568.05

CAR LOAN:       $6,620.77

STUDENT LOAN:   $2,293.24

xxxxxxxxxxxxxxxxxxxxxxxxxxxxxxxxxxxx

TOTAL DEBTS:    $ 16,482.06

xxxxxxxxxxxxxxxxxxxxxxxxxxxxxxxxxxxx
```

AUGUST 1

Still cutting back. Still cutting down. Still living with less. Since taking my vow of frugality, I am a changed woman! It feels awesome. I thought I'd be down and depressed, but the journey has been amazing and the results feel soooooo good. So, where am I?

1. I love my blog. It's like having my own personal finance media outlet. I feel like I am running a mini online newspaper. I am the creator and editor of my blog. I make all the decisions regarding it. To its credit, my job has let me run whatever the hell I want on there. They didn't even balk when I had a guest blogger post on "ways to catch your man cheating for cheap." I secretly think the bosses were taking notes on that post. But I digress....

I'm not paid extra for blogging but I love it. I do just enough work at my day job on the local desk not to get fired, and spend the bulk of my time blogging. When I'm not blogging, I'm thinking about blogging. When I'm not thinking about blogging, I'm looking at other blogs. It's something career-wise that I finally got right! And I am proud!

My blog keeps me honest with my spending, like a spending journal, but one shared with the world! And now my coworkers often stop me in the halls and share their frugal confessions. One woman told me that her husband was out of work, so they brought in the power company to see where they could cut spending on their electric bill. They've saved almost $200 per month. Wow. Beyond being super happy that she was saving that money (I wonder if I should try that?), I was amazed that she trusted me enough to take me into her confidence. We weren't even friends before, but thanks to Frugalista, now we're connected.

2. I think I am developing a case of bachelorette syndrome. I am single and it's not a problem. I know I checked out an online dating site earlier this year, but I am not looking for love now. Love is going to have to find me. Until then, I'm going to keep doing my own thing. It feels good to be out of the game while I focus on other aspects of my life. The cool thing about getting my finances in order is that I can see progress. I can control it if I put my effort into it. My dwindling credit card balance is a result of that. I am open to dating, but I am so not interested in a serious relationship. I just don't have time to get distracted.

My friend Kay thinks that I work too hard. Says I should spend more time meeting new people. Last month's little health scare was not any fun and I know I need to quit being so uptight about things I can't really control.

For now, I'll just keep my options open for dating. I can't nurture anyone else, what with everything I have going on right now. On the plus side, each boyfriend I have is better than the last one—I may be slowly getting closer to finding the one.

And dating seriously is just too risky right now. I just don't think I can afford to get the calculations wrong…again. Another relationship that doesn't work out would be too much for me right now. I bruise too easily. When I get into a new relationship, I have to face the risk that it might not work out. And then there's the endless replay in your head of what he said, you said, he did and you did. I get tired of wondering what happened or why something didn't happen. These aren't questions I really want to start pondering anytime soon. I have no interest in playing bitter chick music on repeat or melancholy R & B tunes if it doesn't work out. I have enough on my plate that I need to figure out. I refuse to start downloading more vintage Aretha Franklin songs to soothe a broken heart and I refuse to break out Alanis Morissette or Kelly Clarkson!

And for all my banter about wanting to be married, I think that notion needs to go on the back burner, too. Eventually, I want to be married. However, I am not now and I am not sure when I will be married. It's best that I figure out my finances on my own, instead of thinking I will have an extra $50,000 + in salary hanging around in a husband. In time, but clearly now is not my time.

Finances can break up a marriage. I saw what it was like for my parents, who were never on the same page regarding money, or much else. I'm still getting my financial groove.

3. Moneywise, I'm doing okay. I'm still a little humiliated that I have to continue chopping away at my massive debt every month. With every $200 credit card payment, I think, *Damn, if I had just acted more responsibly, I would be saving this money.*

Friends say I need to stop beating myself up about it. And I am so happy when I see my debt shrinking every month. There are a lot of things I can't control, but I can control my spending and my debts. It's so funny, I always assumed having some form of debt would be a permanent way of life, but it's not going to be that way for this Frugalista! So what if I wear closed-toe shoes more often so I don't have to get pedicures every few weeks? I don't spend money at my salon like I used to because I'm doing my hair at home between relaxers. It's still hard for me to believe that I was spending more money per year getting my hair done (about $1,300) than I had in my savings account ($1,000)! That was a problem and I'm fixing it. And I'm proud of myself for doing so. Did I really just write that I spent almost $1,300 a year on my hair? Whew.

4. When it comes to my friends, most of my homegirls are Frugalistas, too. We all know we need to handle our cash flow better. We are professional working women, which is code for juggling student loans, living expenses, having fun and looking good. Occasionally, Vivian and the rest of the party girl syndicate ask me about taking a trip with them, but I just explain that I can't keep up with them—not now. I don't feel embarrassed or bad about saying, "No, I can't afford to go on vacation right now." Everyone has read the memo (and blog posts) and knows that I'm in a different place. They must wonder what I do with my money, because women our age should have money for trips (at least I always thought so), but they aren't judgmental. My friends who are attorneys, surprisingly, aren't traveling like crazy. My friends are still building their legal careers, and none of them work in corporate law, so they aren't making six figures yet, although I know they will soon.

I knew that being a print journalist wouldn't make me rich, but I thought that I would have a bit more discretionary income.

I do have money, just not for traveling. If I keep up with the Frugalista plan, I will get to travel again soon. But if I don't keep up with the Frugalista plan, I will forever be on a debt treadmill. So not fabulous.

5. When it comes to that day job, my industry is going to hell in a handbasket. Boss Lady told my friend Julia that September will bring more layoffs at the paper. Julia landed on her feet with a new television job, so that's encouraging. I'm so glad that we are keeping in touch. She is clueing me in on life on the other side of newspapers. I may have the option of volunteering to take a buyout to leave. It's something I've known was an option for me, but I always considered it something that more senior reporters, who are closer to retirement, would exercise. I read every article about buyouts at different papers and how the reporters are doing afterward.

I have worked hard at journalism/newspapers. But I cannot fool myself into thinking that this gig is going to last for much longer. Nor can I fool myself into thinking I can just pick up another job and everything is going to be perfect. I keep looking at the stock prices of newspapers. A value meal at a fast-food restaurant costs more than a share, and you can supersize it! I keep reading the articles about the state of the industry. The news hole is smaller. Staffs are smaller. There's less international news (boo, hiss!). And most importantly (and worst of all), circulation is down. Low circulation = low advertising = less money. Bad math. It isn't pretty. The problems in journalism are much bigger than my aversion to covering local news.

My friend Ron, who left newspapers in the 90s, remembers flying first class to international assignments back in the day (ha!) and says that newspapers are going the way of the pony express. Ouch. Ron is now producing fashion shows. Hmmm. Now, that sounds like a fun career…except for that whole lack of experience thing.

The last thing I want to have happen is to be out of work without a plan. I am from the Midwest. I know what happens when the steel plant shuts down. I don't know for sure that my job will be cut, but I do know that we've had a couple rounds of layoffs (with more rumored to come) and that those empty offices are staying empty. We're not hiring anyone now. And the suburban office is, well, out of sight, out of mind from the main office, where the decisions are made.

Seriously. I can't fool myself. I may have to make a major move. I'm worried about my job security and clearly the stress is affecting my health. One ER visit a year is one too many for this Frugalista! As a single woman I have a single income, so I think about that. If I have to leave work, I won't have any money coming in. But I'm starting to think that I can't let that shape my decisions too much. At a certain point, I'm going to have to make a move—whether I choose to take the leap or the company chooses for me! I don't want to keep playing the single card. I'll keep working and keep my eyes open. I am not naive.

6. Family. Mom is definitely on Team Frugalista. She likes that I'm saving money. She's reading my blog. She never complained about my spending before, but she is supporting my new lifestyle. I don't have much of a relationship with my dad; we haven't talked in ages.

My brother got a kick out of my being on TV earlier in the year. He made all his coworkers watch me live at the office. That made me feel really good inside. He doesn't sweat the details of my life too much. As long as he knows I have food, clothing and shelter, he is content with me. My 2-year-old niece is too young to say "Frugalista." I will teach her soon. Auntie doesn't want her darling to be a promiscuous spender when she grows up!

AUGUST 4

When I ran into the multimedia editor at a work reception, I told him that I'm always looking for ways to help the website and to make the *Miami Herald* a better paper. (And I was looking fine, wearing a button-down shirtdress that I bought on sale for $21. I swear, I looked like such a young lady. I gave him my most ladylike smile.) I guess we hit it off, because he recommended me for video training at the Poynter Institute later this month. I will learn how to use a sophisticated video camera and how to use lighting while videoing. I will learn how to tell better stories through video footage and not words. Three cheers for Natalie! The training is almost a week long in St. Petersburg. I have never been sent to a high-level training course for my job before. I've always paid for classes and courses. Was it my shirtdress? My smile? My work? Who knows? And who cares? I'm super excited!

AUGUST 12

I slipped away from work today to do an NPR segment on *Talk of the Nation,* one of public radio's top-rated shows! The same producer who had me on in April asked me back again. I just took my lunch break during that time and drove down to Miami to do the interview. I worked out of the main office for the rest of the day.

Boss Lady and a few other editors are just about over me focusing mostly on my blog, but I couldn't turn down *Talk of the Nation.* "How will this impact your *job?*" they ask now when I want to do media interviews. I think they think of my blog as a side project for me to keep myself busy. I think of it as a way of life. Every time she has hooked me up, Boss Lady has shown this other side, where she keeps her flat-heeled shoes in my ass. I know she has an office to run. I know this. But really, I'm not the only one benefiting here. Having a *Miami Herald* blogger on NPR is good for the paper.

I don't really like doing secret interviews for my blog. I wish there were some value in what I bring to the paper other than covering local news. Blogging should get more credit than it does.

I won't be able to keep up this secret media act. But I can't stop growing my career. I've outgrown my job, which I could possibly lose due to downsizing, anyway. It's every woman for herself. Forgiveness > permission. Anyway, I was so happy that NPR asked me back.

I can't wait until the video training. I am counting the seconds. Surely, the paper could do without my byline for a week after almost 8 years at the job.

AUGUST 17

I hopped a flight to St. Pete. It's my first time here. It's super quaint, with a beautiful pier. We are staying in the downtown area of St.

Pete, which is like a bite-sized city. I love it. I saw some cute restaurants nearby. I am so ready for this change of scenery. Less is more. There's a hurricane watch for this part of Florida, but I don't care. I'd rather deal with the risk of being swirled away in a hurricane than stay back in South Florida. While I'm here, I'm going to be tied up with classes, but I'm going to try to catch up with one or two interns who once worked at the *Herald* but now have full-time jobs at the local newspaper.

At this training we are going to learn how to use Final Cut Pro, video editing software, and how to shoot the best video. Hopefully, when I get done with training, I will actually be able to edit the video that Lillian and I shoot for my blog. I depend on her quite a bit and I need to get my skills up. Also, maybe I can start working in the multimedia department and get out of local news…. Print media has to reinvent itself, so maybe high-quality videos are the answer.

Anyway, I think the training will be invaluable. I'm the only person from my paper here. Another reporter/editor was supposed to come, but because of the hurricane watch, she decided to stay close to Miami. Maybe I'll meet more people, since I'll be winging it on my own. If I eat a meal not included in the training sessions, I have to be sure to keep the receipts so I can get reimbursed at work. I can't have any more spotty bookkeeping.

AUGUST 18

So far, so good with the training. I'm a PC girl, so I'm not used to using Mac computers, but I'm trying to get the hang of it. I think I'm the only person in the class who's trying to improve the quality of a blog. Everyone else in class is shooting videos either as photographers or as writers (mostly features writers) who want to accent their stories on the web with video. Nowadays, the craze is to supplement your stories with a video component on the media outlet's website. It makes more people want to read your work and keeps the editors happy.

Everyone seems interested in what I'm doing, even if it's not the most serious form of journalism. Is everyone else there that "serious?" I just want to get through this training with more knowledge under my belt. I can't run out of this workshop like I did last year, when I took that Flash course. The last thing I need is to waste the company's money and be seen as a bobo among my journalism peers. I have to make this training work for me. There are a few photographers in the group, so they already have a good eye for visuals and shooting video. I'll be sure to be nice to them in case I need some help when we do our class project!

AUGUST 19

Went to dinner with Frank, a former *Herald* intern who is now a reporter at the *St. Petersburg Times*. Aw, it was nice to see him doing so well. I remember when he asked me for help on stories. He was always super talented, though. His byline appeared on the front page more than mine did that summer.

As usual, we talked about careers and next steps. He's thinking about law school. Ordinarily, I would have given him the speech about the power of journalism, but I gave him a high five on going to law school. If you want to try new things, try them. I told him I was thinking about leaving the paper when another round of layoffs and buyouts comes around. I couldn't believe those words came out of my mouth. Just like that.

"I think I could work on my own," I told him over our Indian dinner. Who said that? Me?

"Are you sure, Natalie? It sounds scary. No job?" Frank said.

"Yes, I really believe I can do it," I told him. "I think I understand the online world better than my company does. They like my blog but they are serious about me doing the local news reporting. I don't see a future reporting on local news. Now, blogging and online, yes. I feel I'd be more successful as a person who knows blogging and social media stuff really well, instead of as a newspaper reporter who has a blog on the side. If I don't leave now, when?"

"Okay, sounds good to me," Frank said.

I swear, kids are so easy to please.

AUGUST 20

One of the instructors reviewed some of the video blogs that I shot for my blog and gave me critiques. I need to work on having tight, medium and wide shots for my videos, to vary my shots. I need to get my energy up on camera. I hate that I didn't have the video up yet from my hospital visit. He would have seen my dedication there! Anyway, he liked what I was doing overall and gave me really good feedback. When he's not an instructor here at the Poynter Institute, he's a cameraman at CBS, working on the national desk. He told me I am 3 years away from being good enough to be a guest on *The View!* Talk about a vote of confidence! Three years is a long time, but I like that he thinks that I could grow Frugalista that much.

Everyone always tells you to follow your passion, and since high school, journalism has been my passion. Even though I love journalism, these days I've been most passionate about The Frugalista Files. I could do it day and night. Actually, I pretty much do it day and night. I would like to do it full-time. It's a good brand. (Who said that? Me?) I like having the conversation about money: when it's good to spend it, when to save it. Since I first took the vow of frugality, I've realized that money is one of the few things that I can control in my life, and I like that. I stuck to the vow and I am chipping away at my debt. So what if I don't get a professional manicure every 2 weeks? In the scheme of things, I have a good life.

I wouldn't mind writing about personal finance in pumps (ha) full-time. And I know that I have a good message to share—I want to share it with as many people as possible. In newspapers you have a somewhat limited circulation, unless you write something on the web. But if I focused on Frugalista full-time, who knows the possibilities? I just started it off as a 28-day adventure in trying to manage my expenses and now it's a lifestyle. That I like! Yay! I'm feeling so good. I should check my bank balance to make myself feel better. (Imagine feeling *better* when you check your bank balance!) I don't have to dip into my savings this month to cover my bills, like I used to do (~~too often~~ all the time) last year. Now I can look at my bank account and smile.

AUGUST 21

Training is over and I'm a little sad now that I'm back in Miami. Boy, did I learn a lot. Thank you, Ma Herald. One of my classmates is an editor at a wire service that feeds stories to newspapers and mentioned that they were hiring. The old Natalie would have jumped at the opportunity and sent off a résumé right away. If I'm going to work for a newspaper or be around newspapers, it will have to be a paper I work for directly. Things aren't perfect at my job, but I get the sense most newspapers have the same problems. Furthermore, they are laying people off left and right. If I took another newspaper-ish job, how long would it last? I want a career, not a job.

I called Lillian to let her know some of the cool stuff I learned and how we could use those ideas for my blog videos. I'm all super hyped. That's the cool thing about these training sessions: you leave so energized and ready to conquer the world. It was like a journalism day spa! Minus the massage, steam room, and um, spa. Still, it was nice to be in a positive setting and not the dreary newsroom. I am such a journo-nerd.

I learned how to light a set and how to shoot on the shadowy side of a face. Who knew? Some of my classmates were old enough to be my mother. A few were pretty young. There were a lot of newspaper people, some big markets, some small. The instructor gave special props to the newspaper people in class because he said we have the strictest ethics of all media and it's up to us to decide how we apply video to journalism. We are the ones who will set the standard for the magazines, broadcast and cable stations. That's right! He had me thinking that newspapers were cool again! I almost stood up and started clapping!

It was nice to network with other people who are trying to figure it all out. All my classmates talked openly about the "changing industry." Most of us know that with the final quarter of the year coming up soon, there will probably be more jobs shed. Just a year ago so many journalists had confidence that we had stable jobs. Now all of us know we have at least a 50-50 chance of losing our jobs. We played the what-if game…. What would we do if we lost our jobs? One woman, who is a photographer, said that she would go into documentary film. Now, that sounds sexy. She was one of the standouts in class. I made sure to add her as a Facebook friend. It would be so cool to say that I know someone who shoots documentaries. My what-if? I would probably become a full-time Frugalista. I would write about personal finance and even try to write a book. I would freelance for different media publications and raise my profile. I wouldn't wake up with a knot in my stomach. Hmmm…getting laid off is sounding, I dare say it, tempting!

I thought it was pretty cool that there were people there of all different ages and experience levels—some had been doing the job for decades. Now, that's dedication. I want to be like that when I get older, always trying new things. Hell, I'm like that now. You don't know what you can do if you don't try.

AUGUST 26

Back at the office this morning Boss Lady and another editor gave me a stern talking to about not being focused on my day job. Really? You send me off to video training, which is supposed to be where the future of the newspaper's business is headed, and then call me on the carpet to complain about local news? And we have been filing local news this long and it still hasn't saved the newspaper industry? Sending me to video training had to cost at least $2,000. If the paper wants to spend its money on people just to complain about them when they get back to work, so be it. Oh, yes, and I need to start working the Friday night cop shift.

I have no words. I just nodded and yessed Boss Lady and her accomplice-in-crime editor. I have no fight left in me. Is it wrong to be looking forward to the next round of layoffs? Time for change.

AUGUST 29

The *Miami Herald* and the *SunSentinel*, which are the main papers in Broward County, announced an agreement to start sharing content.

Um, in the Broward County office at the *Miami Herald,* we compete against the *SunSentinel* for content and readers. So, if we are going to start running news articles from the *SunSentinel,* why does the *Miami Herald* need its own Broward County office? The content that the paper will share won't be the investigative or enterprise reporting. It will be government, municipal, political, courts, etc. All the shit I cover.

What's that I see on the wall? Is that…is that handwriting?

CHAPTER 9

September

DEBTS

×××××××××××××××××××××××××××××××××××××××

CREDIT CARDS: $7,370.53

CAR LOAN: $6,333.30

STUDENT LOAN: $2,244.21

×××××××××××××××××××××××××××××××××××××××

TOTAL DEBTS: $ 15,948.04

×××××××××××××××××××××××××××××××××××××××

SEPTEMBER 1

Well, would you look at those numbers! I am making slow but steady progress. Holla! I'm less than $16,000 in debt! I've been so focused on paying off those rancid credit cards that I didn't even notice that my car and student loan numbers are going down, too! There's a definite end day on installment loans.

I'll feel better when they are less than $7,000. I'll feel really great when they are completely gone. I'm giving myself a mini high five in my head. I haven't starved. I still have friends. I still have a roof over my head. Someone remind me, why was I such a spending slut?

SEPTEMBER 3

I switched all my Listserv accounts from my work email to my personal Gmail account. I know I'll always have my Gmail. Will I always have a work account? No guarantees.

Word around work is that any day now the buyout/layoff offers are coming. That was the word at video camp last month. There I met some other reporters who work for the parent company that owns the *Herald* and they had the current dish on the state of the company. Also, whenever one newspaper parent company starts laying off, the rest follow. Sometimes I think we all work at the same place. When Gannett lays off, McClatchy and Tribune reporters had better pay attention.

We also have a little underground railroad of news WE can use. Journalists move around for their careers, starting with their college internships. After a few short years in the business, and after attending some national conventions, you can pretty much have a contact in several newsrooms in your field. I know my friends and I from different metropolitan papers have been burning up our instant messenger nightly, comparing notes. Between reading the industry blogs, chatting with the assistants and janitors in the office (they look at all the paperwork getting sent around or thrown out) and keeping up with the company stock price, you can get a good snapshot of what's going on. The more we are smart about the changes, the better prepared we will be about our next moves. My favorite journalism Listserv used to have announcements about job promotions, news coverage and job openings. More and more, people are sharing information about industry trends, layoffs, circulation and career changes. Journalists, unite! There's strength in numbers.

At the *Herald,* the Miami reporters get a lot of the juice first and then they cross-pollinate the info to those of us in the bureau. I still wonder if Human Resources leaks the info to certain reporters to get people prepared for the bad news. We report all news all the time. Some of the news isn't for print. It's for our career.

SEPTEMBER 9

The National Coalition of 100 Black Women, Inc., Greater Miami Chapter, is holding a women's empowerment conference this coming weekend at the Seminole Hard Rock Hotel & Casino. I love the Hard Rock. I don't gamble (talk about a money drain) more than $20 at a pop, but it's a nice little complex of shops, a hotel, clubs and restaurants. I used to go to a sports bar there when I was still throwing money around. Super cuties to be found. Guess who is going to be a guest moderator at the panel? ME! Yay! I can't wait. I'm going to moderate a panel called Dollars and Sense.

The conference is designed for women who want to take their careers to the next level by eliminating emotional clutter that may keep them from getting ahead. It's going to be a day full of girl power! Right up my alley.

I still can't believe that people want me to be on panels. I can't lie. There's a part of me that says I can't believe they picked *me.* Do they know what they are getting? I mean, I got myself $20,000 into debt and I'll be moderating a Dollars and Sense panel?! LOL. I guess they do since I put all my business out there on my blog. I can't wait.

SEPTEMBER 11

I wrote a story about a woman in western Broward County, Florida, who rides her family horse to her job at a restaurant because she doesn't want to pay for gas. This economy sucks. I can't knock the girl's hustle. I went a whole month without getting my hair or nails done. There's gotta be another way to make it in America.

I really love this frugal thing because it's opened up a whole new world to me. My wallet is thanking me. I know it is. I want it all, though. I want to have a lean budget and a fatter paycheck. You acquire so much more that way. No to waste, yes to greenbacks. In time, I'm sure. Meanwhile, more frugalizing, more socializing.

I met my girls for drinks at a local restaurant. It's not a scene, but the drinks are stiff and affordable. Lord knows, I have spent many a day running to South Beach, but sometimes you have to drink local. This restaurant is only 10 miles from my house instead of 20 miles. This restaurant is the kind of place where everyone is wearing their work outfits to play. There aren't many people there under age 45, which is fine with me. Older gentlemen don't mind buying drinks. Wallet damage: $9.38. My amaretto sour left me satisfied.

There was supposed to be some poetry or something after the happy hour, but I didn't stick around. The longer you stay, the more you want to drink, talk, eat, drink, talk and eat, and by the end of the night you end up spending so much money, you could have paid off a light bill. Meh. Frugalista tip: Go out with the girls and have a good time, but quit when the check is still small. The longer you stay out, the more likely you'll be to run up the bar tab.

SEPTEMBER 13

Goodbye, Natalie the spending slut. Hello, Natalie the panelist! Today I was on the Dollars and Sense panel at the conference.

I was amazed at how everyone in the crowd took notes about what we were saying. It's one thing to have someone leave a comment on your blog. It's another to see people in person, hear their concerns and watch their reaction to what you say!

When I discussed my spending fast, everyone in the crowd seemed really amused. They think I have superpowers. Not really. Just super debt. Well, super debt that's super smaller. Yay!

I wasn't too nervous about answering the questions. No one

was asking me to forecast the stock market. I mostly chimed in about money-saving websites (RetailMeNot.com, for example) and served as the savings hype woman on the panel. I'm a pretty harmless character: my advice is to spend less than you earn and stop prostituting your paycheck. See? That was easy.

I took mental notes of everything the panelists said. I learn where I can. One of the panelists suggested that we each spend 3 hours per week taking care of our personal financial matters. At first, that seemed like a long time. Borderline obsessive. After I thought about it, it's not. A couple hours during a weeknight or some time on the weekend to go through bills, balance the checkbook and even check investments and my 401(k) is totally doable—and makes total sense. I recently took a Friday off work to handle Natalie McNeal's personal business. For much of the morning, I was my own CFO. I wrote up mileage expenses from my job for reimbursement. I dealt with some outstanding medical bills. I had to make sure I didn't get ripped off and that those were paid. Insurance companies are NO fun. Trust me. I combed the internet, looking for a lower-rate credit card than my current ones and found one with a 0 percent APR for a year. And I DEPOSITED a money order at the bank. Whew!

All that business took up quite a bit of time. But I felt like I had a clearer financial picture after all was said and done. I doubt I'll spend 3 hours once a week taking care of my business, but I'm going to try to spend about 15-30 minutes each weekday on my personal finances. The other day I called my company's benefit resource center to find out how much of a pension I would receive at retirement—it took all of 10 minutes and I was that much more informed.

SEPTEMBER 15

The *New York Times* ran an article on how finding a financial soul mate is the key to wedded bliss. One expert said that couples should sit down once a week and talk about their money.

One thing I've learned from all my blogging is that money sure does have a way of affecting everything in our lives. I cut my travel drastically this year because I'm doing the Frugalista thing. If I were in a relationship with someone who valued traveling, I'm sure he and I'd be butting heads right now. My parents were so not on the same page about money (or much else) and we know how that worked out! Sometimes people blame spending money for the relationship problems. Even if my mother was a total miser like my dad, I still think their marriage would have fallen apart. But their different attitudes toward money were definitely a factor.

What kind of person would be my financial soul mate? He could be frugal, but not cheap. If he didn't buy me an engagement ring, because he wanted to save money for a down payment on a house, I'd have a major problem with that. So sue me. I'm a girl.

I often wonder if how much a woman earns impacts how desirable she is to men, just as the reverse does for women. Yes, men love a pretty face, but I'm convinced that some men would love to be with a woman who is banking cash. Shoot, it's hard out here. I firmly think modern men don't mind a sugar mama. I know one of my guy friends has refused since college to date a woman making less than $50,000. He always has a girlfriend, too. I haven't cracked $50,000 yet in my career. Not surprisingly, he and I have never dated. I'm not mad at it. We all have our don't-date lists. I like to date guys who don't smoke weed!

SEPTEMBER 16

So, another email went out from the paper's publisher. Buyouts/layoffs are here. SHOCKER! If you are approved for a buyout, you will receive 2 weeks salary for every year that you've worked at the paper. For me, that would be 4 months of pay. My health insurance would be covered at the same rate for 4 months. My last day would be October 3. I wasn't targeted to be laid off but I could volunteer to leave and get the package. *Oh, snap, Natalie. It's here.* Time to make a decision.

Do I take the buyout and brave it solo, or stay here and hope for the best?

Why I shouldn't take the buyout:

1. *No steady income. Nothing beats direct deposit, especially when you're paying off massive debt.*

2. *No job. Though, honestly, losing my job seems inevitable at this point. I could easily see myself getting laid off in the next round of layoffs. There are no guarantees that if I get laid off at a later date, I will get the same severance package, or any severance, for that matter. I've read that oftentimes the severance packages get smaller as layoffs continue at companies.*

3. *How can I keep fighting off my debt monster without a real job? Why did the economy have to tank now, just when I'm getting my financial groove? If I have a steady job, those nasty debt numbers at the top of each month will be gone within a year and a half, two tops.*

4. *I have a lease on my apartment. Breaking it would cost me thousands because my rent is $995 per month and my lease doesn't end until April. Staying in Florida, paying rent would cost me thousands, too. The buyout package is nice, but that money won't last very long. After taxes, it's just under $10,000.*

5. *The **Miami Herald** is a good name. Period. I would be leaving that behind. It's been a security blanket for so long. What would life be like on the other side?*

At my company, there's only one major difference between taking a buyout and getting laid off: People who take the buyout volunteer to leave the job and have to get their buyout bid approved by management. People who are laid off are forced to leave. Either way, you are leaving the company, whether by choice or force.

Why I should take the buyout:

1. *I could be a full-time Frugalista. I could call my own shots. I've toiled long enough. I want to do what I want to do.*
2. *I could freelance for different publications. My byline would be all over the internet. Google Natalie McNeal and my name will pop up thousands of times! Working full-time makes it hard to freelance. Also, the bosses aren't overjoyed when they find out I've been writing for other sites. Most of the freelance work I've done is for different departments at my job. I want to write for the world.*
3. **No more buyouts/layoffs looming.** *Watching your friends get fired takes its toll. And you're always wondering if you're going to be next. One ER visit is plenty for me!*
4. *I can become a new media journalist. No one knows where newspapers and other print media are headed, so why not look to the future? If more people are using the internet to access information, it doesn't make sense to work at a print product. I've been working in print my entire career. Those skill sets aren't leaving anytime soon. It would be nice to be in a cutting-edge industry and not in one that's dying.*
5. **It's lonely at work these days.** *My closest friends at the paper have either left the business or are working in Washington or other cool cities. If I took the buyout, I'd be a free agent—able to explore other opportunities and possibly new cities, too.*
6. *Time to take a risk. It's always been school, internship and working for the man. I have a decent résumé, but I don't think it's overly unique. Ouch. It hurts to write that but it's the truth. I need to do something to make me stand out.*
7. **Even though I still have debt, I got this debt with a consistent work history.** *Maybe I need to switch it up a bit. I feel like the frugal thing could go to the moon. It's already*

helped out my wallet. Can I pursue it full-time and still put food on the table?

8. **I could write a book.** *There, I said it. I'm not the quickest writer. I get easily distracted. But if I worked from home, I could actually focus on a book project. It's a journalist's dream to have a book. Dreams? I remember those....*

9. **I hate working the Friday night shift.**

10. **I will be my own boss.**

11. **I'm ready for everything to be about me.**

SEPTEMBER 17

I called my brother, Mac, to get his advice. We are such opposites. He's Mr. Levelheaded. I'm Ms. Passionate. He's worked at the same company since college. I've moved twice since leaving college and have no problem moving again. They like him at his job at a tire company, where he's worked his way up to being a manager. I get treated like a wayward house pet at my job: sometimes lovable, other times a problem. I started at the job as a reporter. And I remain a reporter.

He owns a home. Yeah, I don't even own my car, much less a house. He drinks sporadically. Um…I've learned to drink in moderation. He married his college sweetheart. I dissed a dating site! He's a parent. I'm an aunt (but 1 day I'll be a parent). He enjoys life in Tennessee. I wish Miami had a bigger downtown. He eats lima beans. No comparison for that! And we grew up in the same house!

Me: *"Mac, so I'm thinking about leaving the desk job."*

Mac: *"Really? What brought that on?"*

Me: *"Things are a little weird at work. Lots of layoffs and they're offering buyouts now. I've played it pretty straight for the most part, but I want to try some new things. I think it might be time for change."*

Mac: *"Well, you only come this way 1 time, Natalie. When your mouth is fed, your family is fed. Keep it moving."*

Mac hath spoken.

SEPTEMBER 18

So, I've decided to give it a go! I am going to try to keep The Frugalista Files at the *Herald*—I'm not ready to go indie with my blog just yet. So I'm going to ask the multimedia editor if I can keep my blog if I leave. I pray he's open to it. If I get approved for the buyout but get to keep writing my blog for the *Herald,* that would be a win-win for me. The paper would get fresh content. I'd use the *Herald* name. If he gives me the green light, then I'm O.U.T.

If the editor says that he wouldn't let me keep my blog, then I may have to stay at the paper. I'm just not ready to go independent with my blog yet. I need some consistency.

SEPTEMBER 19

The conversation with the multimedia editor went well. He seemed a little bit shocked that I was seriously inquiring about leaving. "Where is this coming from?" he asked. I gave him the script about how newspapers are changing, and how I fear what will happen next. I feel the need to do something drastic. I don't know what the future holds, which is true.

I refrained from telling him that I want to be UP and OUT. I didn't tell him that I feel like I've been cast as an extra in the movie *Groundhog Day.* I forgot to mention that I hate working the night shift on Friday nights and the paper is messing with my social life.

I can behave when I want to behave.☺

He mentioned some other "entrepreneurial journalists" that he had met who are doing fine without working in mainstream media. He was pretty encouraging. Works for me.

SEPTEMBER 21

Went to a comedy show with Vivian and our girlfriend Cassie, who was in town from Atlanta. Because I was such a faithful customer of the comedy club (check my credit card debt), the club gave me 4 free passes to see a performance. There was a 2-drink minimum.

I told the girls how I'm trying to get out and do my own thing. Think I'd like to give the freelance life a year. If I end up destitute after a year, I'll get a job. I remember watching *The Suze Orman Show* on a Saturday night (I'm such a wild child) and she said that if you are less than 35 years old, do whatever it takes to pursue your passion to build your career. For so long I thought I *was* following my passion by becoming a newspaper journalist, but now I know it's just not for me. Now, when it comes to blogging, I absolutely love it. When Suze speaks....

Cassie and Vivian were really supportive. Vivian has worked at the same company since high school. She's on my team because I'm putting a 1-year time limit on freelancing. Cassie said she had a coworker at her old telecommunications job who launched a website dealing with taxes (go figure) and was doing just fine. Cassie's had a few careers, the latest being a flight attendant. Talk about a reinvention: from a phone industry job in an office to flying in the air. Out of all my friends, I figured they'd be the most agreeable to my new plan. They don't sweat the details much. We just want to have a good time. As long as I don't tell them that I'm going to stop going out, they will support me in whatever I choose. We social butterflies must stick together.

Oh, and for the 2-drink minimum, I made one of mine bottled water, saving $8.

SEPTEMBER 22

The multimedia editor said I could keep writing my blog if I get the buyout. He is a kind, kind soul. Well, that and my blog makes the website look good. Either way, yay! Three cheers! Operation Up and

Out! I put in the paperwork needed to get approved for the buyout package.

On the downside, I got a $200 bill from my July hospital stay. The hospital bill is the gift that keeps on giving. First I paid $300 and now I owe another $200. Ugh, health care is so expensive, *and* I have insurance! Initially, I was going to pay off the $200 bill in $25 increments on a payment plan from the hospital. But now I'm just going to pay the whole thing off. If I'm leaving work, I don't need any more bills hanging around. I can see myself forgetting to pay that $25 bill one time and the hospital putting it on my credit report. I refuse to get jammed up. I'm juggling enough bills as it is. Someone always wants my money.

I'm glad that I'm able to pay it, and that the amount is not outrageous. So many people aren't that fortunate.

SEPTEMBER 25

I went to a free Jazmine Sullivan concert tonight. I needed a break. I found out about the free concert from the Giantstep.net website, which highlights cool artists.

I had the night of fun and fabulous frugality planned perfectly. I closet shopped, wearing the magenta-colored dress I bought this summer for my journalism convention. I wore my favorite rhinestone teardrop hoop earrings. The concert doors opened at 10 p.m. at the Delano Hotel, so I arrived around that time. Because it was early for a South Beach night, I found $3 street parking. I made sure to RSVP early for the event, so there was no bouncer drama at the door. I walked right in. Yay! Drinks at this free event were inflated, running in the double digits for even a beer. I swear, establishments get you at the bar. Miss Jazmine didn't come on until after midnight, but I made a vow not to buy any alcohol. I wanted the night to stay as close to free as possible.

Luckily, I met my friend Brian at the concert. He bought me 1 drink, which was kind. When Jazmine finally came on the stage, she did her thing. I enjoyed her crooning. I stood up and started jamming to her song "Need U Bad." And then it happened. Between my grooving, my favorite earring FELL TO THE FLOOR in the dark, packed room.

Before my frugality vow, I would have chalked up the lost earring to the social game. Earrings, IDs, cell phones are casualties of the night life. But I had NO intentions of buying any new earrings. Acting like a bat, I developed a sonarlike quality, searching for the glistening hoop on the floor. Dark venue be damned! Sure, I might have elbowed a few knees of some folks in the room, but I was a woman on a mission. I needed that earring way more than the Delano did! Buying another pair would have set me back about $20! After about 15 minutes of searching, I found the earring. It was under the table where I was jamming. Whew! Disaster averted.

At the end of the night, I walked to my car and drove home. How much did I spend, total? $3. Operation Frugalista accomplished!

September 26

When the editor accomplice told me that I was buyout approved, I almost hugged him. Yay! Operation Up and Out. I never told Boss Lady I was putting in for the buyout. I wasn't sure if she would be supportive, pissed off or a combination of both. I can never read her and I have years of trying under my belt. I'm sure she knows by now. I'm not sure if I'll hear from her. I'm leaving, so I'm not of any use to her anymore. That's how business works, right?

Another friend at work was approved for a buyout, too. It seems like the people taking the buyouts are getting younger and younger. A quarter-life retirement? Anyway, have fun finding someone to work Friday nights! Or not. It doesn't matter to me. Either way, *I* won't be working the night shift anymore. October 3 is my last day.

News travels quickly in the newsroom. Shocker.

Said my editor: *"So you're just going to quit?"* (Deuces.)

Said my coworker in the Everglades: *"How can you leave?
You have so much debt."* (Yes. I had debt here and I will
have debt when I leave. What's the difference?)

Said another coworker: *"I would work for you."* (Wow. She
and I don't even talk that much. So sweet.)

Said Teresa: *"You can't move home. That doesn't look good."*
(Isn't that what mamas are for? I have a lot to figure out.)

Said a senior reporter: *"That would freak me out, leaving
work without another job. I fought hard for my position
and my pay here. They are going to have to drag me out."*
(If I had your position and salary, I would never leave.
But I don't. You cover corrupt international governments.
I cover, basically, what I'm told to cover. Some jobs are
dead-end. It's a job I can walk away from. Really.)

Said the office assistant: *"You need to do your own thing."*
(Heehee. She's witnessed too much.)

Said a copy editor: *"You get to go on a new adventure and
control your destiny. This is the best!"* (Wow. I never
thought of it like that. I love you!)

SEPTEMBER 30

It's my final week at the paper! Although my desk needed a good
cleaning after all my years of working here, it took me only 30 minutes to pack up and make it spotless. Operation Up and Out motiva-
tion is nothing to mess with!

Everyone is being super nice. No belittling, no digs. So warm.
So fuzzy. For the other reporters, my leaving is a good thing. Because
I'm leaving, there's one less job to be eliminated. The newspaper in-
dustry needs people who are enthusiastic about covering the news.

Everyone who wants their job should be able to hold on to it. If my leaving helps a reporter hold on to his or her job a while longer, good stuff. Or at least that's what I'm telling myself.

I'm just emailing a few people to let them know that I'm leaving to become a freelancer, but my blog will remain with the paper. I'm not telling any of my friends in the media industry about the buyout. I know it sounds crazy, but until I figure out what I'm going to do realistically, it's best for me not to talk about it. I'm taking a leap. A joyful leap, but a leap nonetheless.

One of the editors I freelance for here at the paper says she will make sure that I stay on her freelance list. How awesome is that? I worked with some really cool people. The cool thing about leaving is that I can deal with the paper on my terms, by keeping my blog. Freelancing for editors at the *Herald* who want to work with me is a good thing. It's like *Miami Herald* lite. Fewer calories but more fulfilling. I can dig it. I may need to start wearing *Miami Herald* T-shirts.

Anyway, I'm smiling and humming inside. I may break out in an interpretive dance on my last day. I need to give the peeps here something to remember me by.

Is that…is that a light I see…a light at the end of the tunnel?

CHAPTER 10

October

```
DEBTS

xxxxxxxxxxxxxxxxxxxxxxxxxxxxxxxxxxxxxx

CREDIT CARDS:   $7,173.03

CAR LOAN:       $6,044.64

STUDENT LOAN:   $2,195.13


xxxxxxxxxxxxxxxxxxxxxxxxxxxxxxxxxxxxxx

TOTAL DEBTS:   $ 15,412.80

xxxxxxxxxxxxxxxxxxxxxxxxxxxxxxxxxxxxxx
```

OCTOBER 1

Went to a "retirement dinner" with my coworker Elaine, who also took the buyout offer, even though she's in her 20s. Just the two of us. The buyout has brought us closer together. She's just like me, leaving without another job. Fierce!

Turns out Elaine is a Frugalista, too. She has skin care on the cheap down to an art: she's really good at finding samples of high-end skin-care products. We talked about getting samples of Kiehl's products from the store. Frugalista tip: As long as you don't abuse the privilege, most stores are okay with people getting samples. You could do a few laps around the mall, getting samples from all the fine department stores to last you months.

We went to this cool place in Miami that gives you a free bottle of wine with dinner. So Frugalista. She's an NPR junkie and wants to get into radio. I had noticed that she was always filing radio reports for the *Miami Herald*'s WLRN station. I just thought she was a good employee, and didn't realize she was plotting her exit. I like her style. And she's really good at editing video. Way better than I am. I know she'll get snatched up for a new job quickly. She's a modern newsroom's dream.

As for me, I am going to check out building a full-fledged website around Frugalista to make it more than just a blog and will work on finishing a book proposal. One of my e-homeys said she'd hook me up with her web guy. Her site gets really good traffic.

Anyway, the retirement (ha) dinner was really nice. I spent $13.98 for pasta and half a bottle of wine. Burp.

OCTOBER 2

TODAY. WAS. ONE. OF. THOSE. DAYS. Started off so well. The executive editor called me and said he understood why I wanted to leave and now was a good time. Wow! I really appreciated his call and his "spread your wings, butterfly" message. I know other reporters would be upset that the bosses weren't begging them to stay, but I was happy that an editor was supportive of my decision and wished me well. That's all I could ask for. I wonder, though…does he want to leave the paper, too? It must suck having to chop the payroll. You go into the newspaper business wanting to win Pulitzers, not fire people. Right?

And then…

Boss Lady called me into her office. I got used to being called into her office. And it was rarely for anything good. I had a feeling that she wouldn't just let me slide out the door. We did spend the last 8 years, 5 days a week, together. To let me go quietly wouldn't be… hmmm…emblematic of the "relationship."

Boss Lady gave me a speech about how in the chorus of life (Journalists. Always trying to turn a phrase.) I will need people who can speak on my behalf. She gave me her business card and her cell phone number. Then Boss Lady gave me career advice about what jobs I should and shouldn't take. How I shouldn't take a job covering city commission meetings. Then and there, I flashed back to sitting in those city commission meetings for all those years. The hard benches. The long nights. The paperwork agendas.

"I can't do this anymore. It's over!" I yelled. I started tearing up and ran out of her office. What the hell? I never used to cry. I've spent more time crying this year than I have in the last five combined. Why on earth would I let the words "city commission" from Boss Lady's mouth make me tear up and run out the door?

I know why…. Those words reminded me of my "career that wasn't!"

If anyone had told me that I would be at the *Miami Herald* for 8 years, I wouldn't have believed them. If anyone had told me that after 8 years at the *Miami Herald* that I would be on the night shift on a Friday night, I wouldn't have believed them. If anyone had told me that I would be working in the bureau after 8 years, I would have laughed. If anyone had told me that almost 10 years in the game, and after working at a major market, I wouldn't crack $50,000 a year, I would have spat on them.

Nothing in Miami turned out like I thought it would turn out. Not even quitting a job without another job in place. That's so not me.

I just can't have another career conversation with this woman. We had years of career conversations and they rarely went well; hence, I had a mediocre career here. I don't know if I'm upset at her, myself, the stock market, journalism, my now healed ovary or a combination of all the above. I can't believe I stayed this long. It's ending. It's really ending.

I'm trying to look ahead. I'm done. It's over. My career is mine. The time for "mentorship from on high" is over. I can't keep getting reminded about what went wrong. And for sure, covering the city commission for so many years was something that I firmly put in the "what went wrong" box. I just have to look forward. At this point, it's not about finding another job. I just need to be on my own. I spent the bulk of my 20s at this place. I need to figure out what my 30s will look like. I don't need any parting words. I just need to part.

Why did she give me her business card? I know where she works. I know her cell number. By heart. It's programmed in my mobile. So bizarre. I just want out. No more conversations. We had 8 years to figure it out; an exit chat won't solve shit.

I had been doing so well. My emotions had been joyful, optimistic, hopeful and loving! And now I had a mini-moment courtesy of Boss Lady. Why was I surprised? I want out.

The exit interview with Human Resources went fine. I held it together. I just said I wish I could have done more at the paper. The HR woman gave me a hug and advised me to be careful with my taxes. Le thanks.

OCTOBER 3

Today was my last day. Owww! One coworker who took a buyout is holding a party at a yacht club for everyone at the paper. I invited my college friend Brian to meet me there so I would have someone on Team Nat with me.

The guy who threw the party is starting his own video editing firm. I'm inspired. On its electronic bulletin board, the paper posted everyone who was leaving the paper and a brief bio on them. The local blogger who covers the media in town ran the bios on his blog. Lovefest. The party was a nice send-off. Free drinks. People chatting and thinking about the future. One of the better work parties I've been to. Maybe it has something to do with the fact that so many of us no longer work there!

Everyone asked what I'm going to tell my blog readers. Hmmm.

I do divulge a lot on my blog, but I don't see myself talking about the buyout. With people getting laid off left and right, the last thing people want to read about is me whining about *choosing* to leave my job with a severance package. I'm not going to pretend to be an employee at the *Herald,* but when you're a blogger, a lot of your life is open for discussion and comments. My decision to leave isn't really open for conversation at this point. For the readers' purposes, everything is the same. I'm still blogging in the same place. I'm still doing the frugal thing and I'm going to have to seriously step it up in the savings department. (That dinner and wine jaunt I went on with Elaine needs to be my last supper.) I know people read my blog for the tips on savings and bargains, not for my personal career updates.

OCTOBER 6

Today is my first workday without a job. Last night my stomach was a bit knotted up. I just realized that every Sunday night, my stomach would be in a knot, in anticipation of the workweek. I woke up about 10 a.m., later than usual. Instead of getting ready to leave the house, I went to my computer and started working. In the background, I turned on my television to keep me company. I didn't take a bath until about 2 p.m., opting to work in my sleep shirt. So freeing! I finished a freelance article for the *Herald.* I wrote and posted on my blog. All from the comfort of my home.

Today was a good day. I had no longing to be in an office. No bouts of loneliness. I think I got a lot more work done today. It was easier than it would have been if I still worked at the paper. Weird. I thought maybe I would dawdle a bit because I didn't have a boss looking over my shoulder, but I wasn't chatting to any of my (old) coworkers and was super productive. So far, so good!

OCTOBER 7

Today's random news: Boss Lady emailed me a posting for a job in Chicago. What's that about? Does she want me to leave South Florida and move back home? Does she think I'm destined to be destitute and come begging to her with carpal tunnel wrists and a tin cup for a handout? Was that email her e–olive branch? I think she got the point after our last interaction that we don't really have much to say to one another. Or she should have, rather. I looked the job over. It looks interesting, but I really do want to give this indie thing a shot. I'd like to see if I can make it as a freelancer for 1 year. Boss Lady never ceases to amaze me. I didn't email her back. I didn't want her to assign me to cover a street festival.

OCTOBER 8

Bryant is back in town and took me to lunch at the Hard Rock. When we were walking out of the casino, we ran into some promoters offering $15 to test-drive a Ford truck. My eyes lit up. Well, why not? We got $15 gift cards. I was very thankful for the loot. Fifteen dollars is enough for an eyebrow waxing, a manicure or a meal at a Cuban restaurant. But this Frugalista bought fruit, vegetables, tomato sauce, soy milk and nuts at Publix. Such a bore, right? The tab was $15.24. Shoot, I'm out of work, er, building my brand, and soy milk isn't cheap.

Anyway, tomorrow one of my former coworkers is taking me to lunch. He has a new job doing public relations for a university. Two free meals in 1 week? Leave a job and everyone wants to wine and dine you! Wonder how long this "feed Natalie" period will last?

OCTOBER 10

My former coworker Julia is now working at the local CBS station. She wants me to send my résumé over to her bosses. I guess the TV stations down here like newspaper refugees. I can dig it. We do know how to hustle. It was pretty sweet of Julia to think of me.

Between my freelance work falling into place and people mentioning me to their bosses, I'm feeling pretty good. Even Brian told me to send my info over to his employer. The economy sucks but my friends really have my back. I had been looking for a new job for years, but only now do I think people are taking me seriously.

Normally, career advice is to not leave a job without having another job lined up. I leave my job without another job and more people are recommending me for work! I plan to give this indie thing a year, but it would be foolish not to still circulate my résumé. I need to keep all my options open.

I'm writing another article for TheRoot.com about how to do college homecomings frugally. The inspiration? I'll be missing my college's homecoming because, well, I just left my job. A trip for a party weekend is not something this Frugalista can afford. If you can't join 'em, at least write about it and get paid for it!

OCTOBER 14

Okay, I just noticed something: there's still gas in the fruggie mobile. I left work almost 2 weeks ago and I haven't had to fill up yet. I knew commuting and chasing stories burned up gas, but now that I'm home most of the day, I don't really use my car all that much. I hadn't even thought about that benefit! I'm so enviro-sexy.

OCTOBER 15

Oh, shit. My buyout check came. I had to sign for it at the post office. I was holding a check for $9,683.97 in my hand. Are you serious? $9,683.97? I've NEVER had a check for that much in my life. Never. With $9,683.97 I could buy that Louis Vuitton bag I really lust for. I could pay off my student loan or car loan. I could take a trip to London, Paris or Rome. All three if I planned it right.

So much for fantasies. I drove to the bank and deposited the check. I usually walk to the bank from my house so I can get some fresh air and exercise now that I'm working at home all day. Not this time. Often when I walk to the bank I get hit on by men driving by. I'm not risking this precious check to catcalls and sketchy men.

It's 1 thing to get $1,200 every 2 weeks. It's quite another to get a lump sum of money with no strings attached—the govy has already taken out the taxes.

It took everything not to scream, "I'm rich, bitch!" I know I'm not rich, but I'm just not used to large sums of cash. At the bank I checked out everyone else. Why didn't I wear a trench coat to the bank and place my check in one of the inside pockets? I should have worn shades, too. Carried a briefcase. Where is Inspector Gadget when you need him?

This check was made out to me: Natalie McNeal. And now it's safely deposited in my savings account.

OCTOBER 17

The college homecoming story is live on TheRoot.com website! Who said my living room can't be a newsroom? I'm the hardest working out-of-work person I know. I posted the link on my Facebook page, too. All my college friends had a field day with it, leaving comments and their own homecoming tips on there. Yay, social media. It's so social. I know my girls are going to have so much fun at homecoming. Hopefully, I can go next year.

Even with this buyout money sitting in my bank account, it's not good for me to spend it on a vacation. I need it to pay my rent and I'm not sure what business opportunities will come my way. As my mother always says, "A bird in the hand is worth two in the bush." I know I have this buyout money in my account. I need to hold on to it and not spend it frivolously now, in anticipation of making riches later. I know I have what it takes to make it. But I have to play it smart.

OCTOBER 21

Heehee. The cool thing about blogging is that I can write about stuff and readers don't know that I'm talking about my life. When I blogged about people being offered buyout packages at work, clearly,

I wrote about the pros and cons without mentioning myself. But, um, yeah, I did the research so I could find out the information for my own purposes.

Seems that everyone is anxious or depressed about the crappy economy. It's weird, but now that I'm into this freelance thing, I'm not as stressed or freaked out as I was when working at the paper. I've had time to figure out how to grapple with the stress but without spending lots of money.

Here's Natalie's list of guaranteed stress relievers:

1. **Take a long bath at night.** *I am a big fan of lavender. That scent so relaxes my mind and an extended soak in the tub leaves me feeling renewed, like I washed away my problems. I do some of my best thinking in the bathtub. Showers are invigorating, but sometimes I just like to marinate myself. I don't mind looking like a prune later. I always plump back up.*

2. **Watch reality TV.** *A good old train wreck of a reality show makes me feel great about my life. You get to compare your circumstances to the "scripted drama." I bet you would prefer your life any day. I am super addicted to* The Real Housewives of...*series on Bravo. It's my guilty pleasure and the cast members are my best friends in my head. Sure, they all behave poorly, but don't we all have our moments? I've been told I have a "Nattitude" at times. The girls on* The Real Housewives of...*series let me know that I am not the only one. Since I've been, um, building my brand and working from home, I've been getting more and more engrossed in reality television. I don't have workplace drama anymore, so I have to get my fix somehow.*

3. **Stop talking to grouches.** *I step away from my well-meaning but McGrouchy friends. Some folks are just cranky and gloomy. I do not want to hear it.*

4. **Talk to upbeat people.** *I have a crew of people who have a really positive outlook on life. We don't talk every day, but when I need a jolt of confidence, they deliver.*

5. **Find solutions to your problems.** *Instead of just whining, moping or complaining about a problem, I find solace in finding a solution for it. When I find a workable solution to whatever is bothering me, I feel smart. I didn't go to my college's homecoming weekend this year, because of limited finances, so I wrote a freelance story about college home-comings. Once the story hit cyberspace, a lot of my college friends got in touch with me to tell me how much they enjoyed the piece.*

OCTOBER 22

I was quoted in a *Philadelphia Inquirer* article on "istas." There seems to be a whole brood of us womenfolk using "ista." In the article, the writer mentioned The Budget Fashionista, the name Stylista and me, Frugalista. It's like a superhero name. Me likey.

OCTOBER 23

So I contacted one of my e-homeys' web guys to see how much it would cost to do a major Frugalista website. His quote: $10,000. Um, that won't work for my budget. As much as I want to get in this inter-net game, I've been reading articles about online ad sales softening. If I invest that much in a website, I would need to be guaranteed a return. Plus, that $10,000 would be my entire buyout $$$. I'm a risk taker, but I'm not foolish.

I will have to keep promoting my blog at the *Miami Herald*. My blog and my personality. Those two things are free. Sweat equity is the best start-up capital to have when you are starting out because it's free. I read that on Mark Cuban's blog. Yes, I've taken to reading Mark Cuban. He started MicroSolutions with a $500 advance from his first customer and he's made it. This Frugalista is open to tips from people who have made it work!

OCTOBER 28

So my mother insists that I head home for Thanksgiving. I have to admit, I haven't been around for many holidays. When you live away from home and work in a newsroom, holiday time off is a no-no. Thanksgiving was always a hard one to score because the Friday after was a workday, and everyone, no matter what race, religion or ethnicity, celebrates Thanksgiving in America. It makes no sense to buy a plane ticket for 1 day. I usually spend T Day at a friend's home. I'll bring a bottle of wine or a key lime pie. I'm such a loved orphan. So, anyway, now that I'm out of work, er, building my brand, my mother is insisting I come home. She's even buying my nonstop ticket for $219 on Southwest. I don't have to pay baggage fees, either. To get the ticket to Chicago that cheap, I'm staying a week, beating the high-priced travel days of the Sunday and Monday after the holiday. It will be nice, albeit cold, to be in Chicago for the week. But how often do you get a chance to change your lifestyle? I'm going to blog from my childhood home. Yay. Another cool point about being indie: Wherever there's an internet connection, I can work. The world is my workplace.

The fact that I'll be home for a week will make my mother happy. I'll get to chill out at her house, rather than in a 1-bedroom apartment with beige walls. I never realized how small my apartment was until I started working from home. Before I left work, I was always at work or rushing out to meet friends. Now I'm at the apartment quite a bit. Hmmm. My work schedule at my apartment is just to work as much as possible. I wake up by 10 a.m., and I do a blog post. I read a bunch of personal finance and beauty blogs and comment on the posts that I like. When readers leave comments on my blog, I make sure to post a response. I answer every email in my in-box.

I am surprising myself a bit. I am reasonably accomplished, but I don't always have the best focus. But working from home in the quiet—except for when the maintenance workers trim the bushes at my complex (BZZZZZ!)—I get a lot of stuff done.

I feel very safe in my apartment. It's like a cocoon for creativity, whereas before it was a place to rest my head.

When I worked a desk job, I would drive home at night, pick up the mail and then park in my lot. Now I walk to the mailbox to get my mail. I try to time it so I meet the mailman there. The human interaction is welcome—to be perfectly honest, it's a bit of a highlight during the day. I read all my mail now. No bills are slipping through the cracks on me!

My neighbor, who owns an internet-based educational company, has been really supportive. I can call him during the day just to connect with a person. We both need little breaks during the day. I'm getting to know him better now that I work from home.

OCTOBER 29

I found out on my journalism Listserv that *Ebony* magazine is looking for freelancers to write about Election Day. I emailed the managing editor, saying I was available. I hope I get picked. I'd get national exposure! Plus, this is going to be one hell of an election.

Since I quit, I've been having a bit of an identity crisis. I haven't yet figured out what to call myself and what I do. Am I a blogger? A blogger with a journalism background? Saying I'm a freelancer sounds soo...soo...transient. It makes it sound like writing is a side hustle to pay for a summer trip to the Caribbean. I'm working full-time, just for myself.

I could say I'm self-employed. An independent journalist? I don't really consider my brand of blogging serious journalism. It's opinion, yes. I have ethics, yes. But I don't do a lot of original reporting. (Now, that's journalism.) Hmmm.

Then again, my blog is at the *Miami Herald,* and you can't get more journalistic than that. So maybe I am a journalist still? I am definitely a blogger. I can feel confident saying that. If I cover Election Day for *Ebony,* though, I'd still have some journalism cred. I need to be sure to always commit acts of journalism, i.e., freelance. Ugh. There goes that word again. I mean, I still want my byline circulating.

My friend who is a former fashion editor and has written several books says that I should be focusing on my book proposal and should stop writing articles. I know I should. But I just left the newspaper and I want people to know I'm still around and still writing. I can't let this economy get the best of me. I won't let this crap economy ruin my career, even though I'm not sure what it is these days. Writing is breathing. It lets me know I'm alive. Maybe I'll focus on the book proposal next month.

Okay, okay, I admit it. I'm intimidated by the book proposal. Book proposals are often 50 pages long. I write 300 word blog posts. Still, I have no excuse not to try. I called Alexis, the author, one day to gossip and she basically told me she didn't want to hear from me unless I was working on my proposal. Ouch. No one takes you seriously in the writing world unless you have a book. It's a rite of passage, even if the book is a pamphlet. There aren't a ton of people who can say they are an author.

I can't blame it on being too busy at work to focus on writing the proposal. I make my own schedule now. I control my own time.

The best thing and scariest thing about being on my own: I have no one else to blame if I fail but myself.

OCTOBER 30

Got approved for Election Day coverage for *Ebony*. Reading the email from that editor had me smiling from ear to ear. The magazine wants to cover Obama supporters in South Florida. They won't be hard to find, and years of covering South Florida for the paper has made me knowledgeable about every nook and cranny in the town. I'm taking the game national. Halloween is tomorrow. I can't focus on a costume. I got so much stuff going on. I quit my job but I'm still working.☺

Since I'm definitely doing election coverage, I sent a few more emails to my friends at other newspapers and magazines to see if they need a stringer for the day. If I get picked up by a few more media outlets, more people will see my work and I'll get more money.

CHAPTER 11

November

DEBTS

xxxxxxxxxxxxxxxxxxxxxxxxxxxxxxxxxxxxx

CREDIT CARDS: $6,975.46

CAR LOAN: $5,754.78

STUDENT LOAN: $2,146.06

xxxxxxxxxxxxxxxxxxxxxxxxxxxxxxxxxxxxx

TOTAL DEBTS: $ 14,876.30

xxxxxxxxxxxxxxxxxxxxxxxxxxxxxxxxxxxxx

NOVEMBER 1

At the journalism conference I went to in July, my CNN connect Tanya hit me up to be on the planning committee for a December fund-raiser for the local chapter of my journalism association, the NABJ. Things are heating up with the planning. We want to do a good job so our chapter looks important to the national organization. Plus, it's good to give back to the organization. I especially want to do a good job because Tanya looked out for me earlier this year by helping me get booked on CNN.

So Tanya wants me to send out emails and act as the social committee. We are having a CNN personality speak, hosting an auction and then throwing an after party. Surprise, surprise. I'm using my email lists from my previous parties to reach out to people and setting up a Facebook group for the event. I picked the venue, and because I hate paying for venues, we're holding it at an attorney's big old house. The attorney is a former *Miami Herald* attorney and I've been to his house for a few networking events he has held for local professionals. I thought he would be open to hosting us, so I suggested his name.

Not only did dear, sweet Tanya put me on the planning committee, I have to do an after party for the younger visitors. I mean, the fund-raiser will be lovely, but not like hitting a nightclub. So, I have to find a party spot for an after set. I'll be spending this month finding a place for the after party. The cost to enter this fund-raiser is $50. I really hope that because I'm helping plan this event, I don't have to pay to attend. Considering my new employment status (read: self), I can't really pay $50. It's for a good cause, but I need to be mindful of my budget. We'll see.

At any rate, helping to plan this event is turning into a side job. I'm making calls and getting the lists together. I'll probably have to go to a Saturday meeting. I hate meetings! I have to suck it up, though. The NABJ is a worthwhile cause. No complaining. Furthermore, it's probably good for me to come out of hiding and interact on a project other than Frugalista. I'm a bit Frugalista obsessed. I've already tried to think of a way to meld my Frugalista brand with the event. I don't think giving away a free coupon at the live auction at the party will earn enough money. LOL

Everyone on the committee is working their ass off. It's a good group with lots of connections in South Florida. Tanya knows what she's doing. Mush!

NOVEMBER 3

Okay, so I did something kind of weird today. The beige walls in my apartment were getting to me. I drove to the grocery store...just to hang out. I mean, it's so bright and pretty there. It's so clean. So many people gather there, buzzing about the floor. And the vegetables come in such lovely colors and I got excited each time the little sprayer would wet the veggies.

I have enough food in my home. I just needed a change of scenery. I never thought of the grocery store as the hotbed of activity or fun, but these days I love it.

No, I'm not losing it. I swear.

This working from home thing is a big change for me. A welcome change, but a big change. I think I'm forgetting what the days of the week are because I don't have to be anywhere. Every day is a Saturday, or Monday, as far as I'm concerned. Sometimes I wake up in the middle of the night and send off emails. Every hour is a work hour. People always tease me about my 3 a.m. emails. It's been pretty easy for me to get my work done because I am not getting distracted by office chitchat. I don't have to worry about office gossip. I don't have to answer to anyone but the one editor I am working on an assignment with. I don't have to worry about snarky comments from really anyone. I have my own little sanctuary...with beige walls. All I do is hunker down and work.

Every day I play my Kanye West CDs. I keep reminding myself of my favorite line of his song "Champion: For me giving up's way harder than trying."

NOVEMBER 4

Election Day. Yippee. *Ebony* gave me free rein to go wherever I want to go in South Florida to speak to Obama supporters. They want me to take the pulse of what people were thinking, feeling and doing during the day. Man on the street. Slice of life. This is the election of a lifetime. History will be made if Obama wins. History will be made if McCain wins. I will be able to tell my grandkids that their grandmother covered the election for *Ebony* magazine! I can save the magazine and show them the little nuggets I submitted.

This year's election has been a journalist's dream. I wasn't on the election team, but I did cover a story about an Obama campaign outreach for the *Miami Herald*. And now I get the chance to get a nibble of the election again. Yes, I'm still a journalist. I cannot wait to hit the streets. I've had my TV on CNN all morning long and I've checked out MiamiHerald.com and WashingtonPost.com for news.

The days leading up to the election have been like no other. My spin class instructor at the gym gave a speech about how our country will be different after this election. All everyone does is talk about politics and who will win. As a quasi journalist, I can't really express my political beliefs publicly. Well, at the newspaper, I knew I couldn't. Not sure how it works now! A lot of journalists don't even vote. Still, the magnitude of this election is not lost on me. And I get to have a byline. I'm still in the game!

Before heading out, I fixed myself an egg white omelet with Monterey Jack cheese, broccoli florets and shrimp to give me plenty of energy. I bought the shrimp frozen and in bulk with a discount club membership I share with my mother. I pay only $15 a year for the membership. Working from home is turning me into quite the chef. In my mind, anyway.

By 8 a.m. I was out the door with my notepad and smartphone. I knew I wouldn't have time to drive home and file the feeds, so I planned to file most of the reports from my phone in my car. (Editors LOVE it when you file early.)

I drove north to Fort Lauderdale and filed an early story with quotes from some residents. One woman, Tracy Dunlap, said she hadn't voted in 20 years. "When (Bill) Clinton was president, everything was good, and then Bush got into office and everything went to hell," Dunlap said. "I don't want 4 more years of the last 8 years."

Dang, sista! Twenty years without voting?

Next, I went to Liberty City in Miami. I talked to a lot of people and was surprised to find that a lot of them flew in from other states to help get out the votes for Obama because Florida was a battleground state. Then I headed north to Miami Gardens, which is between Miami and where I live. Everyone was super kind when I interviewed them. I'm not used to that kind of treatment. Then I realized I was representing *Ebony* and not a mainstream newspaper. Whenever I went into those communities as a *Miami Herald* reporter, it took a little extra work to break down the walls. But, go to black communities and say you are from *Ebony* magazine, and folks treat you like you're their niece!

Warm smiles, pats on the back. Such a different experience. After I left Miami Gardens I drove to a suburb next to mine and then returned home to eat and take a shower. I burned up quite a bit of gas, but I wanted to do a really good job so *Ebony* will hire me in the future. Sometimes you have to spend money to make money. You can't do man-on-the-street quotes from your home.

Later on, I met Vivian and Cassie at an Obama election party at the Gulfstream Park Racing & Casino. I pulled some of my Chicago connections to get myself, Cassie and Vivian on the list (I mean, I WAS covering elections). We got in. No problem. The manager sat us in VIP, but we didn't get any of the free food there. Cassie said we should try to get in on the grub, but I didn't want to push. We didn't have to pay to get in. Food, clearly, wasn't an option.

When CNN called the election, the crowd roared. People started hugging each other. Men were misting up and crying. My cell phone blew up with text messages, which I couldn't answer. I was working! While everyone gets to enjoy history (or mourn it, depending on your orientation), journalists have to document it. I just soaked it all in and filed more feeds to the editor.

America had its first black president, Barack Obama, and I can now tell my grandkids that I covered the election. I hate that my maternal grandmother wasn't alive to witness this.

The *Ebony* editor emailed and said that she liked my feeds from Election Day. What a confidence booster! Looks like I didn't spend all those years running the streets of South Florida for nothing! I can't wait for the stories to hit the magazine.... I know all my mother's friends and cousins are going to read them and give Mom a call. She'll love that.

NOVEMBER 5

I'm writing about how Michelle Obama is a Frugalista. I have tried to stay away from politics on my blog, because it's best for me to stay neutral. However, now that the First Lady is a Frugalista (she closet shops and shops at the same affordable stores that I do), I have a right to write a blog post.

So awesome that a Frugalista is in the White House, and she's from the South Side of Chicago, where I was born. Every time I see her wear that canary-yellow J.Crew cardigan, I smile. If a millionaire can wear her clothes more than once, who am I to spend frivolously? I wonder if I would ever see Michelle Obama at the mall? What would I say? Then again, I probably wouldn't say anything. I don't want the Secret Service to jack me!

Yep. I know I'm going to get good traffic off that post. Some of my readers from London left comments. I didn't think about them reading my blog to get an insight into American living/thoughts/sentiments. No pressure. None at all. LOL

A few of my regular blog readers emailed me and we chatted about the election. They are my electronic pen pals and I hope we meet one day. I told a few of them in an email that I had left the paper. They all gave me a virtual high five, wishing me luck.

NOVEMBER 7

So my friend Carly, who nursed my wounds during my birthday weekend earlier this year, came to town with our childhood friend Renita. I picked out an affordable party girl hotel for them to stay at in South Beach, called the Whitelaw. Carly and Renita have been BFFs forever. I picked Carly up from Miami International Airport about noon. I can do things like pick up friends now that I'm the boss of me.

Carly looked great when I picked her up. I haven't seen her

since I crashed on her couch during my birthday weekend. She was starving and wanted to get a bite to eat right away. I was game for a good lunch. Financially, I'm doing pretty well since leaving work, and lunch is always more affordable than dinner. I don't really spend money anymore. I grocery shop (I mean, the grocery store is my new hangout spot) and I cook at home constantly. I've pretty much turned into a nonconsumer.

I picked the cute Ethiopian place near downtown Miami. Because it wasn't in South Beach, the place was affordable. I ordered a salad. It was nice sitting there in the sun, chilling, eating with my friend without worrying about the next place I HAD to be. Carly and I grew up together and we went to the same college. And we have WAY too much party girl history together. In high school we used to party at Chicago's North Side clubs, like the Riviera, until way past 2 a.m. We have photos of us all dolled up in front of some tacky spray paint backdrop. Ah, memories.

She has had a "work break" before, opting to leave her first job after undergrad, and even worked as a bartender when she was in between jobs. Nowadays, she's a web producer and she helps my writerly self with all the tech stuff I have yet to understand about my new online work life. Carly paid for lunch, which I greatly appreciated. I could have afforded it, but maybe it was her way of thanking me for not making her catch a cab or SuperShuttle to the hotel. Or, maybe she's just sympathetic to my plight of doing the independent thing.

After lunch, we went back to her hotel to wait for Renita to get in. I found metered parking right next to the hotel. I think I'm getting good at avoiding the parking garages. And good thing, because they're expensive in South Beach. When Renita finally made it to the Whitelaw, the hotel was having a happy hour from 7 to 8 p.m. with free drinks. Yay. Frugalista power. Renita, Carly and I sat outside and had a couple.

And then…the bartender working the main bar inside, a little con artist with an adorable accent, called us over to his bar, where two Englishmen were drinking. "Ladies, ladies, why are you sitting over here by yourself? Beautiful girls should be over here," he cooed. "I will take care of you."

My Frugalista antennae should have been raised. The bartender was too nice. But we went, anyway. Mr. Bartender started with the martinis, Patrón, rum. Whatever we wanted, he poured. He even whipped up his house specialty, which couldn't have been all that special, seeing as I can't remember it now. The two Englishmen, brothers, were rather gorgeous. Renita danced on the bar. Whenever I drink, I turn into a piglet. I started ordering appetizers. And drinking. And eating. And drinking. I think Carly was really bonding with one of the guys. They were pretty easy to talk to. I greeted them with a "Cheerio." They told me I was too cute to sound like Mary Poppins. Oops. Heehee.

And then I started doing my bar seat wiggle, grooving to the music, throwing one hand in the air and rolling my shoulders. I know enough not to drink, stand up and dance. I do it all from my bar stool. Those drinks—the ones I remember—were damn good. I had no intention of spilling one drop. All the while, like a little devil on my shoulder, the bartender kept saying, "I will take care of you."

Lord. I knew the bill would be a mess.

And it was.

With several rounds of drinks, I knew the bill for our tab SHOULD have been more than $300. But, we ended up at $150, wink, wink. We had to break the bartender off with an über tip. The old bartender hookup scam. If only we had stayed with the free drinks!

Damage to my wallet: $70. Damn, you, bartender with the cute accent.

I was in no condition to drive home, so I spent the night with Carly and Renita. Someone was looking out for me; I didn't get a parking ticket.

I love my homegirls, but I can't afford to party this weekend. Friends are always coming to Miami to pick up cruise ships, get away to South Beach or attend conventions, so I get to entertain quite a bit. And entertaining in Miami doesn't mean a walk on the beach. It means clubs, drinks and restaurants. And that's money I just don't have.

Sometimes I think living in a tourist destination makes it harder to manage your money. I wonder how many people who are locals in other tourist destinations think they would be rich if friends never visited? Maybe if I never drink another drop of alcohol, I could be rich? Hmmm. But then I wouldn't be Natalie.

NOVEMBER 10

Yippee! The Oxford University Press named "Frugalista" a finalist for word of the year. I got beat out by the word "Hypermiling." Boo, hiss! I am so excited. The OUP even gave a link to MY BLOG when describing the definition of a "Frugalista:"

> —*person who leads a frugal lifestyle, but stays fashionable and healthy by swapping clothes, buying second-hand, growing own produce, etc.*

Who knew when I started blogging that I would get this kind of attention? One minute I was the girl being told that my blog should get the ax and the next minute I'm getting shout-outs from OXFORD.

NOVEMBER 11

So, I met with a party promoter today for the swanky nightclub Karu & Y for the fund-raiser "after party" that I am in charge of. He says he will give us speedy entrance to the club (yay, no velvet rope bs) and we'll get armbands for 2 free drinks. I made sure to let him know that we would be having CNN personalities and media executives in town. My ass is on the line with this party. I cannot deal with any Miami club life foolishness. He said he was glad that I met him in person. He seemed earnest and businesslike. Miami clubbing is not for the faint of heart. Every bouncer thinks he is a superstar. People act funny about the lists. Hopefully, since I went to the vice president at the club, he will send the message out to his staffers that my guests need to be treated well, with no door drama.

Helping to plan this fund-raiser is definitely more work than I anticipated. I pray it goes well.

NOVEMBER 20

I submitted a holiday gift giving guide to a reporter who I hope will use some of my tips for an article she's writing. In true Frugalista spirit, most of my ideas are centered on experiencing the company of a loved one. That's what the holidays are about, right? I suggest that going to museums and boat shows (if you're in Florida) and volunteering are fun ways to spend the holidays. As for me this holiday… hmmm. Only Madison, my niece, is getting a gift. I found her some adorable pink Timberland boots for $40 at Nordstrom. It's kind of wild that I would spend $40 on a pair of boots for a little girl when I don't even spend that much on my own shoes these days! When it comes to the niece, though, I am a sucker. I can't wait to see them on her wee feet. I wonder if I should start an auntie fund for gifts for the munchkin? I think my niece has the ability to turn me into a poor woman. I love her that much!

NOVEMBER 23

Speaking of gifts, my friend's wedding is today. She's not a traditional bride. Instead of registering at a department store, she has a website asking everyone to donate $50 for the honeymoon in Hawaii. Well, really, I paid $51.50 for the wedding gift. The website had a processing fee! I've never been to a wedding that had a suggested gift amount. I've never been to a wedding with a processing fee. I was going to spend about $50 on the gift, anyway. I like to give people what they want, even if it comes with a processing fee.

Hmmm. My friend may be onto something. It's not like she needs another toaster. I'm sure she'll enjoy a trip to Hawaii much more. I'm sure there will be at least 50 people at her wedding. I bet she won't have any (or will have very little) honeymoon debt. I'm not mad at her. It's not like I had to spend $9.99 on shipping a gift from a department store to her home. Just a $1.50 processing fee. If I had just paid her in cash, I would have saved $1.50. Bad Frugalista! HA!

BTW, I'm wearing the magenta dress! It's my go-to dress!

NOVEMBER 24

High five to me. The *New York Times* top word man, William Safire, named "Frugalista" his word of the year. He mentioned my blog in his post. That's the second time that I got a shout-out from the *New York Times*. I'm so excited. I got quite a few emails from my old co-workers and other journalism peeps for that one. I emailed Safire to thank him. I was SO scared to email him. I didn't want him to edit my grammar. LOL. And it turns out that he has a Yahoo! account. I guess he's not full-time at the paper. We are so in style—workers with no corporate email!

Off to Chicago tonight to see Mommy for Thanksgiving. Gobble! Gobble!

NOVEMBER 26

So, work never stops. I wrote an article for TheRoot.com on how layaway has come back with a vengeance and is all the rage this year. This crappy-assed economy has people paying for items over time and not all at once. Credit cards are not en vogue like they used to be, so stores like Kmart and Sears are pushing layaway to move merch. I got to do a WashingtonPost.com live chat about my article. I can't believe it. The *Post* has a smart readership, so I felt a bit intimidated, but there was no way I was going to let fear stop me. It's one thing to freelance for TheRoot.com, which is owned by the *Post*. It's another to host a live chat on the *Washington Post's* main site.

Because I'm at my mother's home in Chicago, I used a laptop in her bedroom. At first the chat started slow; then people started asking questions. I got zinged a few times by "chatters" who had to put in their two cents, but I stayed the course. All in all it worked out and now I can say I've been on WashingtonPost.com. Yay!

My favorite question:

Olney, Md.: *Simplicity is indeed making a comeback. Sears and Kmart, among others, have resurrected the layaway option. For those who have weak credit or are not in good financial shape, this option allows them to be frugal but still be able to afford higher ticket merchandise. Do you think layaway will give customers some economic freedom and [help them] become better consumers, instead of slaves to massive credit card debt?*

Me: *Yes, frugal living is all the rage. I think layaway is good for people who are in a financial bind and need to buy essentials, like warm winter coats or boots. It certainly has lower fees than most credit cards, so that's a good thing. However, you have to be careful that you are putting items on layaway according to your payday. If you have to budget that hard for an item that's not an essential, then that's a problem.*

After writing that, I had a reflection of the year before, when I decorated my apartment in anticipation of the Youngster, er, Man X's visit. True, my apartment needed some decorating TLC, but buying a 6-foot-tall fake tree on credit probably wasn't the best way to spend my money. I had lived for years in a sparsely decorated apartment. Saving up for a few months to decorate my apartment would not have hurt me. If I had paid cash for decorating my apartment, I would have a lower credit card bill now. I am very thankful that I was able to leave my job, but it's not lost on me that I have a lot of bills to pay and I am running on borrowed time. That buyout money was not enough to put me into retirement. The credit card payments nibble at my money every month.

If I had had zero debt when I left the *Miami Herald,* I could have coasted financially for a really long time. I can't wait until I'm debt free. I'm just trying to keep the faith.

NOVEMBER 27

Thanksgiving dinner at my cousin's house in the city. When my mother let the older cousins know I quit my job, the room was suddenly quiet. I let them know that I left with a package and that I'm doing just fine being self-employed.

Ugh. It's so hard to tell people who survived the Great Depression AND lived through the civil rights movement that you actually quit a job. They fought hard to get jobs, battling segregation AND a crap economy, and here I go, quitting my good job. I had benefits, steady pay. I didn't have to dig ditches. Looking back, I probably could have done some things differently at work.

I pray my cousins don't think of me as a quitter. I know they'll love me, anyway. The civil rights movement was about getting access and leveling the playing field. Well, I had access and left it. Doesn't sound so good when I write it. I don't have any regrets about leaving but I know I have to keep working hard. I will make them proud. I always have. I am just taking a different turn in my career. Sometimes you have to take a risk to create more success for yourself, right?

NOVEMBER 28

Black Friday. I'm staying in the house. 'Nuff said.

NOVEMBER 29

I went ice skating in downtown Chicago with Carly and Renita. It was only $10 for skate rentals. Carly's dad took Carly and me to the metro station and we rode the train downtown and met Renita at the ice rink. She lives a short bus ride away. I hadn't been ice skating since I was like 8 years old. And I skated like it, but I didn't care. It was just cool to be out there tiptoeing around the rink. This part of my life, I'm doing what the hell I want to do and I'm not going to worry a lot about what anyone thinks. I felt like a little kid again.

CHAPTER 12

December

DEBTS

xxxxxxxxxxxxxxxxxxxxxxxxxxxxxxxxxxxxxxx

CREDIT CARDS: $6,777.60

CAR LOAN: $5,463.71

STUDENT LOAN: $2,096.94

xxxxxxxxxxxxxxxxxxxxxxxxxxxxxxxxxxxxxxx

TOTAL DEBTS: $ 14,338.25

xxxxxxxxxxxxxxxxxxxxxxxxxxxxxxxxxxxxxxx

DECEMBER 1

My gym membership ($36 per month) allows me to go to any gym in the national chain and there's one in the next burb from where my mother lives. So my mom and I went to the gym today. We did the elliptical, did squats with the medicine ball and lifted weights for our arms. She was a champ! Getting healthy—eating well and working out—is part of the new life I'm creating for myself. No more excuses that I work long hours, so it's hard to work out. I make my own hours now. Cooking at home more and eating out less sure help, but working from home keeps me from moving and I want to de-pudge a bit. My mother never works out. I have had a $36 per month gym membership for ages and I'm the first to admit that I don't use it nearly as often as I should. Frugalista tip: It doesn't matter how good of a "deal" you have on your gym membership—if you don't use it, you're wasting money.

Since I'm not shopping like I used to, and neither is Mom, going to the gym is a good activity for us to do together. It's wild to me now how shopping together was such a big part of our relationship for so long! Whenever I came home for the holidays in previous years, my mother and I took the train to downtown Chicago and hit up all the stores on the Magnificent Mile. After shopping for hours, we had lunch at a Thai restaurant. Shopping in downtown Chicago is such a lovely experience.… Seeing the Christmas decorations on State Street. People watching at the Water Tower. Watching all the little girls dressed like dolls and their mothers going into the American Girl shop. Eating caramel and cheese popcorn from Garrett Popcorn. Looking at all the cool street art. Listening to the street musicians playing an instrument for a dollar. Le sigh.

Oh, well. It's foolish for us to do any shopping now. Mom's retired, and I'm retired from newspapers. LOL. Downtown Chicago isn't going anywhere anytime soon. Plus, I tend to buy quality items (I shop more at Banana Republic than I do at H&M), so my wardrobe is doing just fine right now. My clothing is holding up style-wise and quality-wise.

I've taken to becoming an expert closet shopper. And now that I don't have to go into an office every day, I don't even wear much of what I own. I can pretty much get away with wearing a sundress or romper while working from home. I am clothes coasting. My closet has me cruising.

For the first time in my life, I can honestly say I need nothing. I have everything.

DECEMBER 2

The National Bureau of Economic Research has made the official declaration: we're in a recession. Um, really? You think? Every company is shedding employees like cheap fur and this is the profound statement we get? The newly unemployed called this ages ago. Meh.

I packed tonight because I'm heading back to Miami first thing tomorrow morning. The fund-raiser party is in 2 days and I have to make sure everything is in order. Mom and I had a great visit with each other. Normally, she and I would be on each other's nerves after spending a week together. In her heart, I think she secretly wants me to move back home. She didn't want me to move home before without a plan, but now that Frugalista is doing well, she's okay with me back in the abode. Fair enough. But I want to ride out the Miami thing. I can't break my lease and, anyway, I like having my own place and space.

DECEMBER 3

Back in town. I'm excited to be back in Florida and figuring out the rhythm of my new life. If all goes well, maybe I can find a way to live in Chicago for part of the summer and then Miami in the winter! That's how the real players do it: 2 residences! They're called snowbirds. I feel like there's no cap to what I can do. It's up to me to make it happen. I am determined to create the life I want. No more complaints or excuses.

I put the finishing touches on getting ready for the fund-raiser tomorrow. I want to be sure to look good. I know I am going to see a lot of the top editors and business leaders from the South Florida community. It's always good to put your best foot forward. I bought a sexy tube-top, A-line dress. I broke down and bought the dress new for $75 at Nordstrom. I mean, I am on the planning committee—I have to look the part. Now that I work from home, I am taking my time getting ready. Vivian agreed to do my hair for free. Yay! She really is a jill-of-all-trades. I didn't want to spend the $35 for a wash and set. I get my hair done only when I need a relaxer. She roller set my hair and it looked fantastic. I suggested that she think about coming to the party, but the $50 ticket price was too steep for her. Yeah, I hear that.

DECEMBER 4

Okay. The fund-raiser was SOO awesome. We rocked it. Really, we did.

We started the night with a mix and mingle with an open bar and appetizers at the attorney's house. Then the CNN personality Roland Martin gave his speech about covering the election. Afterward, we had an auction.

I did some serious networking. I ran into Denise, who worked for *Nightly Business Report*, a national PBS show based in Miami. We judged a writing competition together for the NABJ a few years ago, but I didn't know her well until that night, so it was great to hang out and get to know one another better. Denise introduced me to her boss. I wondered if my dress was a bit too revealing to meet a business editor? Maybe I should have worn a pinstripe suit?! Hee. Oh, well. It was pretty cool of Denise to make the introduction.

I had stopped by the nightclub in the morning to get our VIP armbands. The club gave me like 200 of them for my guests to wear later at the after party at the nightclub. Oh, my. I knew we wouldn't have a crowd that huge at the door. What would I do with all the extra armbands? I couldn't sell them on the black market, could I? I protected them like they were a bag of gold, hiding them away in a bedroom at the venue.

Between the ticket sales and the auction, we raised more than $8,000!! The auction committee did a great job. I can pack your party but I don't have the corporate hookups to get donations. I was really impressed with the goodies. We auctioned off a pair of Air Jamaica tickets, spa baskets and hotel stays. I kept my hands by my sides the whole time, since I couldn't afford to bid on any of the prizes. Jamaica sounded divine, but I know my limits!

After the fund-raiser ended, we hit the club, Karu & Y. I asked one of the party photographers to take a picture of me. I wanted a professional quality photo and since I was in full makeup and Karu & Y is one of the sexiest clubs in Miami—it is absolutely gorgeous—I wanted to capture the moment. The photog showed me the picture and it was gorgeous. He promised to email it to me. He was super sweet. He was just happy that I got him in the club for free. One Frugalista favor deserves another.

So, anyway, there is a Studio 54 disco-theme party later in the month at Karu & Y and I'm going. Old Natalie would never have gone to a disco-theme party. New Natalie says she only comes this way in life one time. The guy who got me the hookup at Karu & Y apparently throws it every year. Now, what will I wear…?

DECEMBER 9

Tanya hit me up for the $50 for the fund-raiser. Ack. I drove the check over to her house. The last thing I need is everyone knowing that Natalie shafted the organization by not paying the entry fee. Tanya is quite the bill collector. I don't know what to think. On the one hand, as members of the planning committee, we should be the first ones to pay to get in. There are no free rides. On the other hand, I can see how paying for tickets to receptions, fund-raisers and whatnot can really add up. Is it unreasonable to be comped for the event for planning it? I'm working but I don't have full-time work. I guess I pick and choose what's important to me. This is the biggest event that I've done for the organization and I had a hand in making it a success. It's not an annual affair, so that's cool, but I can't afford to be a free party planner. Especially now that I'm freelancing and working from home—my time literally is my money!

Note to self: I'm going to need to start itemizing my taxes. I can see how these affairs will be a line item in my budget. These are the things I need to think about now that I'm indie.

Then again, that's the way business gets done. Anyway, paying the $50 was the right thing to do. I think of the $50 as one-fourth of my pay from writing an article for TheRoot.com. Ugh.

I can't wait until I get to the place where paying for charity/fund-raising events isn't a concern. No one likes a social leech who can never pay for or contribute to anything. Do I really need to spend my money eating an expensive meal, or do I need to spend it at a fund-raiser that benefits my profession?

Think, Natalie. Think.

DECEMBER 10

One of the online editors at the *Miami Herald* asked me to visit the Salvation Army and do a story on the finds there.

At the Fort Lauderdale store I found—but didn't purchase—some good buys:

- *A red Betsey Johnson cocktail dress for $59.99, originally $330.*
- *A Gucci credit card holder, brand-new, for $50, originally $150.*
- *A platinum engagement ring for $550, originally $1,800.*

Yay!

The media contact at the store told me that the best way to get the good stuff at the Salvation Army is to make friends with a sales associate. Let her know what you're looking for—a little black dress in size 10?—and she can call you when one shows up. I had no idea, but clothing at the Salvation Army goes on sale, too. A discount from the seriously discount place! Fancy that! On the right day, you can find what you're looking for. Golf clubs. Vintage furniture. Fur coat. But you have to be a smart shopper. I may add the thrift store to the list of places I check out when shopping, but I'm always going to keep Nordstrom and my designer discount stores on my shopping rotation. I've learned the hard way: don't buy something just because it's on sale. Nineteen dollars here. Twelve dollars there. Those purchases add up and make a big dent in your budget. Frugalista tip: It's all about buying what you need, not what you want or think you want.

I still have the Coach bag I bought in college, and I've recently started wearing it again since my DKNY purse took a beating. And yeah, that Gucci bag I begged my mother to buy me as a shortie, it's in the rotation, too. It's vintage. (Wink, wink.)

DECEMBER 12

A *Los Angeles Times* reporter called to interview me for an article about Frugalistas replacing fashionistas. I told her that frugality is all the rage and that popping bottles of champagne in nightclubs, spending money on useless stuff are soo, soo last year. Heehee.

She asked me if I had given any thought to writing a book, and I told her that I had, but I needed to do a proposal. "Get that proposal done over Christmas," she crowed. Eeek. *Focus, Natalie! Focus.* While I'm still coasting on this buyout money, I need to make my time off work for me. Anyway, the reporter also interviewed the Oxford University Press, which made the word "Frugalista" a finalist for the word of the year, for the article. Go *L.A. Times.*

DECEMBER 13

Holiday party tonight! The one thing about hanging in a professional crowd is that there are always lots of parties. Journalists, attorneys and teachers groups all host holiday parties. Especially in Miami, where partying is a way of life.

Tonight my friends coerced me into going to a toy drive holiday party for some local attorneys' association. You either paid the $20 admission fee or brought a toy for an underprivileged kid. I just can't afford to spend crazy money during the holiday season, but I gave in. I found a Dora the Explorer puzzle to bring to the toy drive and was let in for free. I hope the kid who gets my toy is a brainiac who loves to do puzzles. It's not an electronic game, but it's what I could afford to give.

The party was nice. It was held at my favorite neighborhood restaurant/bar. A lot of the people who attended my party during the summertime were there, so that was nice. All my closest friends were there. We just ate finger food and sipped on drinks. I'm feeling pretty thankful. I am always going to their attorney functions. I could be the mascot for the South Florida legal profession. LOL

DECEMBER 15

So my cousin Robert, who teaches at Le Cordon Bleu cooking college, asked me to speak to his students about living frugally. Now, that's something I know about.

I swear, Robert has the best job! As soon as I got there, I was offered some delicious lobster that some students had just learned to prepare. Then, when I got to my cousin's class, there was a plate of lasagna waiting for me. Oink! Before I said a word about being a fabulous Frugalista, I had eaten enough food to last me through the next day. I could get used to this. Um, lobster and lasagna as part of your school curriculum—these students are already a step ahead of the rest of us frugal-living-wise! I bet they spend a lot less on dining out than the take-out aficionados.

The students were sweet and receptive. I talked to them about frugal living and saving money. I warned them about getting into credit card debt. One said he shops at thrift stores because the clothes are so soft from being already worn. Wow. I never thought of that. Three cheers for the student Frugalisto in class. I need to make sure my cousin gives the kid an A.

I also talked to them about blogging and how important it is to have an online identity nowadays to further their careers. It's not enough to become a great chef. Nowadays, people would rather eat at a restaurant of a chef with a kick-ass website. People judge you by your online presence and the online reviews of your work. At least younger people I know do.

It felt good to get out of the house early in the day and interact with people. I still wander around the grocery store when I need a change of scenery, but it was great to speak to people instead of staring at vegetables!

DECEMBER 16

Essence.com ran 3 of my tips in its online holiday gift guide. For its "25 Fun & Free Creative Ways to Give" article, the writer picked up my idea of making a DVD of all your family photos and my tip about volunteering as a family or visiting a museum on the free days. While talking to the reporter who interviewed me, I thought I could write this story in a heartbeat. Shoot. I hear *Essence* pays its freelancers pretty well.

I behaved during the interview and the writer was super sweet. This brand building is no joke. I can already tell in just over 2 months after leaving work that I'm changing. All I do is obsess over the brand and obsess over new opportunities. I practically wanted to ask the freelancer if she knew of any writing gigs. Now, that would be bad form.

I'm a weird hybrid of a reporter and a blogger personality. I write to pay the bills for now, but I think the brand is what's going to give me a career. Everyone says it's better to have someone else write an article on you, because it gives you credibility. If I'm going to give this Frugalista thing a serious go, I'm going to have to learn how to transition easily from being a writer to a person that offers a service. It's not all about the money. Being quoted on Essence.com is nothing but an honor. Sometimes I will have to put on my reporter hat to make money. Other times I will have to learn to give the quote, which, essentially, is better for my brand. It's a whole new way of thinking.

DECEMBER 19

I went wig shopping today. Heehee. Tomorrow is the Studio 54 party at Karu & Y and the new, more adventurous Natalie couldn't be more excited. I found the most Foxy Browneriffic Afro wig at the flea market for $20. This wig is GORGEOUS. It looks just like human hair. I went to the fabric store and bought some green ribbon to tie around my wig. I'm wearing some ancient platform shoes I already own—don't ask (shopping binge back in the day)—and a green and gold maxi dress that I bought last year. $25 for a costume that looks SHAZAAM certified! Not bad.

Mina, who is a prosecutor, said she'll go with me. She didn't tell me what her 70s costume would be. I know what I will be. FABULOUS!

The photographer from my fund-raiser after party emailed me the picture he took earlier this month. I love it. I'm going to put it on my Facebook page. It's my new hot mama photo.

DECEMBER 20

Disco, baby! The party was hot. Everyone was patting my 'fro all night! Heehee! Mina didn't wear a costume, which was fine with me. I stood out even more! I made sure to let Gerry, my contact at Karu & Y, see me. He approved! He was fly in a white suit. Aw, toot, toot! Aw, beep, beep! I'm posting the photo taken on my blog!

DECEMBER 22

I'm done with Christmas shopping. My munchkin niece got $40 boots. La madre got a light winter jacket. I bought my brother a Best Buy gift card. Total spent: $140. I would have been more than chipper to not exchange gifts but my mother loves gift giving—and receiving—at Christmas. In years past, when I suggested waiting out Christmas, the idea didn't go over too well.

The consumerism associated with Christmas is overwhelming. I love giving gifts. I like making other people happy. I'm known for picking out the perfect thoughtful piece, but all of that comes at a steep emotional (and, yes, financial) cost if you can't afford it. It's called that January credit card statement! Santa's buying friends and influence! Never trust a man who makes you sit on his lap and ask for favors. Santa is not fooling me.

DECEMBER 23

Mom's in town for the holiday. She's staying with me in my 1-bedroom for a month. We will be around each other nonstop in my apartment. She comes every year, but in years past, I was working most of the time. Maybe this will be a time where we can get to know each other better. After all, I'm in a happier place, doing my own thing.

In other news, in the mail was an invitation to TheRoot.com inauguration ball in January. Whenever a new president is elected, there are tons of balls to celebrate the swearing-in ceremony. I most certainly have never been invited to a ball in my life! Wow. That's some Cinderella stuff! Ugh. I would have to get the invitation the year I quit my day job. I'll figure something out. I'm not sure if I can make it, but I so want to go. How often do you get the chance to go to a ball celebrating the nation's first black president? Pretty sure the answer to that is *once in your life*. If only my money could catch up with my career! I'd be the fiercest.

I don't think I've worn a ball gown since, um, my high school prom. And actually, I wore a long gown for junior prom. For my senior prom, I wore a short dress because I wanted to show off my legs.

Oh, I so want to go! It's not like I have to worry about getting time off work, heh.

DECEMBER 25

My mother made fun of me today. She gave me $100 as a Christmas gift. I ran to the ATM to deposit it into my account. On the Christmas holiday. She was like, "I don't know why you are going to the bank. It's closed." Clearly, this woman has never worked freelance a day in her life. A check is worth more in the bank than in my living room or purse. Shoot, anything can happen. The days of Natalie misplacing and losing checks are OVER!

So, Christmas was pretty low-key. Lots of calls to family members. Mom said she liked the coat, although I wonder if she was a bit miffed that I didn't have it gift wrapped? I hate wrapping paper. It's wasteful and time-consuming. I don't buy that many gifts, so why do I need a whole roll of something taking up space in my apartment? It's the thought that counts, right?

Mom basically made the dinner: Cornish hens, fresh green beans, corn bread and dressing. I popped a bottle of my favorite *moscato*, even though my mother doesn't drink. More for me. I didn't help out that much in the kitchen, as my mother likes to rule that area of the home, even if it's not her home. I was happy to let her do her Christmas cooking.

I posted a Christmas blog post. I wanted to send my peeps some cheer. I had already emailed a few of the readers I've connected with off-line and sent them their e-cards.

It's Christmas day and I can't help but think of where I was this time last year. The bills were piling up. That January credit card statement loomed on the horizon. I was stuck reliving the same bad day at work, over and over again, waiting for things to change. And the spending—oh, the spending. I was on an endless bender of reckless spending. And now look at me. I, Natalie McNeal, am actually advocating spending *time* with family instead of spending $$ for the holiday! I like to think I've come a very long way.

I am blessed.

DECEMBER 26

So, I decided which one of the many New Year's Eve parties I'll go to. (LOL—I sound like such the socialite!) In past years I went to this criminal defense attorney's NYE party with a $20 cover, but not this time. He has a gorgeous pool, good champagne and plenty of food, but I always see the same people. And I can't see paying $20 to party in his backyard this year.

Miami is strange sometimes. People really do charge their friends to party in their backyards. I partied so hard at his last party that I dropped my cell phone in a cup of Hennessey and Hypnotic. That little oops cost me $250 for a new cell phone!!!!!!!! Lord, I have come a long way. I cannot afford another mishap with the go-hard party scene. Janet, one of my former coworkers, said that there's a free party at a club we can go to. Now, that's a more Frugalista way to bring in the New Year. I'll be there!

DECEMBER 29

Got an email for a freelance assignment from an editor at the *Miami Herald*. True to her word, she was giving me some work. I've known her since I was a college intern at the paper and she was an education reporter. I'm so glad she has my back. These days it's so exciting to get assigned stories.

One thing I'm realizing about this freelance way of life is that if you don't have decent relationships with people, you starve. A lot of my work has come from people I've known for years. My TheRoot. com hookup came from a college friend. I told a fellow blogger, Patrice, about my "new life" and she offered to let me write briefs for her alternative newsweekly. It's $40 a pop. That's good money. Sign me up!

While I haven't felt comfortable enough to send blanketed emails to my Listserv groups about my taking a buyout, I've been letting key people know that I'm open for business. Every day I comb my journalism Listservs looking for writing opportunities. I still have a cushion with my severance package. I am in a good place.

I've been spending a lot of my time at the computer during Mom's visit. She says all she hears is clackety clack from my keyboard. Clackety clacking is how I put food on the table, Ma McNeal!

So she wouldn't feel like I was ignoring her, I let her in on my supersecret potato recipe and we made it together. Okay, so really, my childhood friend gave it to me on Facebook, and nothing is secret on Facebook. But it is still damn good.

Preheat the oven to 450°F. Wash and slice at least 2 potatoes, medium thin.

Put the slices on a foil-covered baking sheet. Toss the potato slices with extra-virgin olive oil, garlic salt, pepper and Lawry's Seasoned Salt.

Slice a small lemon and randomly put the slices on top of the potato slices. Pull the leaves off a few fresh oregano stems and place on top of the potatoes. Cover the potatoes with foil and bake until tender, about 25 minutes, checking every 10 minutes.

DECEMBER 31

Wearing black slacks and a black tank top to the party tonight. My mother helped me blow-dry my hair super straight, so it looked good. Mom stayed home, as she does every New Year's Eve. She's quite the homebody. The party is going to be pretty laid back, so I don't have to be in a cocktail dress. And it's not in South Beach, which means free parking. I'm meeting the girls at the club. And I am ready to welcome in the New Year!

JANUARY 1

Happy New Year! Party last night was tight. I got in at 2 a.m., which is SUPER early for me. I met Mina, my friend who is a prosecutor, and one of our guy friends at the spot, too. My mother was like, "Oh, you must be getting old. You're getting home so early." Boo. Hiss. And why wasn't she asleep? She just wanted to hear my party tales!

I'm still a party girl, just a party girl who brings herself home at a decent hour with money in her pocket (and her cell phone in her purse). The later you stay at the club, the more you drink and the sloppier you get. Meh. That's *so* not Frugalista.

Anyway, the cost of my New Year's Eve party: gas to get there. That was it! Yay!

Wow. January 1. A new year. This last year has been crazy! Last January I thought I had met someone special, a close friend was dying and I was deep in debt. Well, the bad news is that I lost that someone special and my dear friend. The good news is that I've also lost a chunk of my debt. Oh, and I left my job. I really do feel like the world is open to me as I carve a new career.

That debt. What a burden. I was more than $20,000 in debt, and now I've whittled it down to less than $14,500. And I'll keep chipping away at the money mound until it's nothing. Yes, I am proud of myself. When I think about how I changed my life and my lifestyle, how I was filling up time shopping and spending money…whoa.

And this year? I still traveled and went out with my friends—and looked good while doing it. I learned to style my hair and still have a full head. I stopped getting mani-pedis every 2 weeks and my feet are still attached to my legs. I have plenty of clothes in my closet. I quit my job and found my passion for writing by becoming a full-time blogger, freelance writer and brand builder. I even got invited to an inaugural ball in D.C. Frugarella to the ball?!! Ha-ha, maybe.

I can't wait to figure out what this new year will bring. I'm not quite sure and that's part of the thrill. The one thing I've learned for sure, I'm over being a spending slut. Decreasing debt is a better thrill!

This year I have to finish my book proposal. It's mandatory. No more excuses. I want a book deal. As a journalist, I'm so used to telling other people's stories. What about my story? I want to take Frugalista as far as it can go. It's my therapy, best friend, love, financial partner. It's not often that you get to do things that you love. I just want to do more of it. I don't think I have everything all figured out, but maybe that's the exciting part. Everything in my professional life before this was thought out and planned. What if I just see where I can take life? I'll keep working, building my brand, being open to new opportunities and then I'll see where I land. I've given myself a year. If I'm still breathing this time next year (and not living at home with Mama McNeal), I'll consider myself a true Frugalista success. 2009, here I come!

EPILOGUE

Okay, before you start demanding your money back, yes, I did become debt free, just not in a year's worth of time. It didn't even happen in 2 years. It took me 2 years and 4 months before I was debt free.

My money mantra during those lean months after leaving my full-time job and turning into a full-time Frugalista: I will only invest my money, not spend it! I only allowed myself to spend my limited income—or even use my charge card—if I felt it was an investment in Frugalista.

I blogged like crazy. I blogged so much that I pretty much didn't shop anymore. I was beyond frugal. Over the following year, a lot of my clothing took a beating because I wore it so much.

Frugarella did go to TheRoot.com inaugural ball and inauguration ceremony. I figured that I would get some face time with editors who had given me much-needed work. And because I made my own, ahem, work hours, I could take off to see the new president sworn in. I tried to find some freelance work covering the inauguration, but every journalist in the world had put in dibs for that assignment! LOL

I did another no-buy month in February and it got a lot of media attention. This time, a producer from CNN asked for me to be on the air. I didn't even have to pitch myself. I was on CNN 4 times that month and that raised my profile quite a bit. A crew even came down and did a story on my lifestyle, which was super fun.

As you can tell, I did get the book deal! A Facebook friend (yay, social media) recommended a literary agent and she guided me through the book proposal writing process. It took me 2 months to get the book proposal done. I locked myself in my apartment to get it done and didn't even see my friends. My agent shipped off my proposal to several publishing houses and we found a home at

Harlequin, which shouldn't be a surprise. Harlequin is very girly and my book editor, I do believe, is a Frugalista. She is young and knows all the good sample sales in New York. It was meant to be!

I got some more good news over the next year. Denise, who attended the journalism fund-raiser that I worked on, called me and said that her job at *Nightly Business Report* had a grant position she thought I'd be good for. Well, I got the job, but instead of working at the job for a year, I had to finish the work in 8 months. Perfect! I had only $300 in my account by the time I set foot in the office to work.

I couldn't have created a better dream job for myself as a contract web producer at a national business show. It had a beginning, a middle and an end, which I liked. The people at *NBR* really understand how business works. They talk about stocks like they are their children. (How's Disney doing?) LOL

I was worried that the job would turn my Frugalista into a side hustle and I really wanted to focus on Frugalista full-time. But I needed the money. Luckily, working at *Nightly Business Report* made me a stronger Frugalista blogger. I finally learned how to edit video properly. I also got to edit two senior journalists who blogged for me. Can you imagine that? Me, editing a journalist who used to work on the *Philadelphia Inquirer* business desk? I also got to advertise my project with bloggers and in the business press, so I got to work with a budget a bit. I booked personal finance experts, too, so I got to pick really smart money people to help me with my project.

Anyway, at *Nightly Business Report,* I was asked to sit in management meetings, which was a new experience. While my job was mostly web based, if I wanted to work with a correspondent for a story on the air, the bosses gave me the green light. If I knew someone who would be good to put on the air for a commentary, the bosses made sure to give them a shot. I loved feeling valuable.

While at *Nightly Business Report,* I got an offer from Kmart to do professional blogging for them. Getting that blogging trademark for Frugalista (thank you, Marlon) was one of the best investments I have ever made. I am the featured blogger at Smartshoppersunite. com, a social networking community made up of mostly women who love to talk about the best way to find deals. That job is also a dream job. As part of my job, I get to visit Kmart stores and pick out clothing for shoppers that are Frugalista approved: easy to wash, can be worn many places, really affordable and look damn good!

When I got the Smartshoppersunite.com gig, I had to leave the *Miami Herald* blog platform. The separation was amiable and I'm so thankful that they let me continue my blog after I wasn't a full-time reporter there. In the end the bosses there gave me what I really needed from the paper. I am very grateful to them—even to Boss Lady—for helping me initially to keep my blog going when I needed it most.

So, finally, after more than a year of all my blogger friends urging me to take my blog on my own, I went indie and launched Thefrugalista.com formally in December 2009. So I worked at *Nightly Business Report* and Smartshoppersunite.com at the same time. Let's just say, I got two big girl checks. I used one check to live on and the other check to pay off my bills. I picked one bill a month to pay off. I paid off my credit cards first. Then my car. And then my student loan. By April 2010 I was debt free. Yay!!!

So, the moral of this story: work smarter, harder and never be afraid to take an educated risk. It pays off.